Post-Christendom Studies

Volume 8—2023–2024

Contents

TAYLOR MURRAY AND LEE BEACH
Editors' Introduction — 4

TAYLOR MURRAY
The End is Nigh?: Religious Affiliation in Canada's 2021 Census Data — 6

SAM REIMER
When the Saints Aren't Marching In: Disaffiliation, the 2021 Census, and the Cultural Zeitgeist in Canada — 14

ANNA ROBBINS
More Buddhists than Baptists? A Call to Reframe Baptist Discourse for Mission in Canada — 21

STUART MACDONALD
Through a Clear Window: The 2021 Census Helps us See Christianity in Canada Today — 27

JAMES TYLER ROBERTSON
Happy is the Land that Robs from God: Secularizing Canada in the Mid-Nineteenth Century — 36

JAY MOWCHENKO
Embracing the Possibilities of Resurrection — 48

MARK NOLL
Prospects for Christianity after Christian Hegemony　55

LYNNE TAYLOR
Learning From a More Secular Future: Insights
From Aotearoa New Zealand　62

DAVID TARUS AND JOSHUA ROBERT BARRON
Home Away from Home: An Outsiders' Reflection
on the 2021 Canadian Census　74

MARK J. CARTLEDGE
Religion and the Canadian Census Data: Some
Reflections from Across the Pond　85

LEE BEACH
The 2021 Census Panel: Reflection and Response　93

Book Reviews　97

Modern Authors Index　111

Senior Editors
Lee Beach
Gordon L. Heath
Steven M. Studebaker

Assistant Editors
Dudley A. Brown
Taylor Murray

Editorial Board
Najib G. Awad, Hartford Seminary
John E. Franke, Second Presbyterian Church of Indianapolis
A. J. Swoboda, George Fox Evangelical Seminary
Joel Thiessen, Ambrose University

Post-Christendom Studies, a peer-reviewed academic journal produced by the McMaster Divinity College, publishes research on the nature of Christian identity and mission in the contexts of post-Christendom.

Articles are posted on the McMaster Divinity College website and at the end of the year, the volume is available in hard copy as well. Manuscripts should be sent to mdccpcs@mcmaster.ca.

Copies of the printed version can be ordered from Wipf and Stock Publishers (wipfandstock.com).

Content of *Post-Christendom Studies* is copyright by McMaster Divinity College, Hamilton, ON, Canada. For more information about McMaster Divinity College, visit: www.mcmasterdivinity.ca.

ISSN 2561-4738
ISBN 979-8-3852-2880-5

Editors' Introduction

Taylor Murray
Tyndale University, Toronto, ON, Canada

Lee Beach
McMaster Divinity College, Hamilton, ON, Canada

Those readers familiar with *Post-Christendom Studies* will note that this edition of the journal is a little different from those that have come before it. In light of the recent publication of the 2021 Canadian Census data—which showed a significant decline in Christian affiliation—the editors decided to dedicate the bulk of this edition of the journal to a "panel" discussion on the state of the church in Canada. In short, it is a scholarly conversation on the changes that have taken place over the past decade and beyond. It includes contributions from academics and ministry leaders from a number of different contexts, from Canada and elsewhere in the world, and it integrates interdisciplinary perspectives on the past, present, and future of Canadian Christianity. Five essays include perspectives from within Canada, and four include those from outside of Canada. We hope this will be a helpful resource for pastor, parishioner, and professor alike.

Before proceeding, it is important to note what this edition of *Post-Christendom Studies* is and what it is not. Put simply, church leaders seeking easy answers on how to minister in post-Christendom will not find them here; what they will find, however, is a rich discussion on the ever-evolving context of Canadian Christianity and how the reality of the church's place in the Canadian context may also provide a vehicle for reflection on the role of the church in other Western contexts as well. Understanding these changes (and what caused them) will be crucial for the church in the days ahead. It seems highly improbable to expect these numbers to reverse in any significant way. Post-Christendom is here to stay in Canada (and also in many other places)—the church must determine if it is ready and willing to meet these challenges.

In addition to the panel discussion, this edition of the journal also contains several book reviews on recently published works that deal with the topic of post-Christendom. This collection of reviews (printed alongside the panel discussion noted above) shows that *Post-Christendom Studies* continues to be a forum for conversation on contemporary Christianity in Canada and beyond.

The End is Nigh?:
Religious Affiliation in Canada's 2021 Census Data

Taylor Murray
Tyndale University, Toronto, ON, Canada

Introduction

Anyone with even a passing awareness of the church is likely familiar with the trope of the pastor who points toward the day's newspaper headlines to find proof of the approaching apocalypse. In that recognizable imagery, he (because it is often a male pastor) searches for evidence of when the world will end, how it will end, and who will remain, among other questions. When Statistics Canada published its latest (2021) census data on religious affiliation, some Christians may have felt a similar sensation.[1] Across the theological spectrum, the data showed evidence of a significant decline in Christian affiliation. As with the pastor with newspaper in hand, one might ask: could the end be nigh?

In academic circles, few (if any) were shocked by the trend in the census results. In fact, nothing in the data came as a surprise for those who have been paying attention; the numbers have been trending in this direction since at least the middle of the twentieth century. As Brian Clarke and Stuart Macdonald have documented, there has been a steady decline in "Christian affiliation, membership, and participation" that began in the 1960s and has continued

---

1. All data from 2011 and 2021 in this essay are from Statistics Canada, *National Household Survey* (2011), and Statistics Canada, *Census Profile, 2021 Census of Population* (2021). Available online: www12.statcan.gc.ca. It also draws on material from "The Canadian Census: A Rich Portrait of the Country's Religious and Ethnocultural Diversity," *The Daily*, 26 October 2022, 11–16. Component of Statistics Canada catalogue no. 11-001-X.

into the present.[2] The speed and severity of that decline were both yet to be seen, but with the latest round of data, perhaps we have a clearer picture of the future of Christianity in Canada.

Post-Christendom Studies invited a panel of scholars and church leaders to evaluate and reflect on the data published in the census. The next nine papers record those observations; five of them are from Canadians, and four of them are from observers outside of Canada. In order to provide a backdrop to that discussion, this brief introductory essay identifies some of the major "headlines" we find in the data, including the decline of Christian affiliation, the growth and stability of other religions, and the rapid increase in the number of "nones" (those who select "no religion" in the census). This essay explores these topics individually to get a sense of the direction of religion in Canada.

Decline of Christianity

As noted above, the story of Christianity in Canada over the last ten years (and beyond) is a story of decline. While the national population grew from 32,852,320 to 36,328,480 people, Christians dropped from 22,102,745 to 19,373,325—or 67.3 percent of the population in 2011 to 53.3 percent in 2021. Not only did churches lose the battle against population growth, but they also struggled to retain members they already had, either because people were leaving the church or because older members were dying.

A closer look at the individual Christian groups shows how significant the decline over the last decade was. According to the data: Catholics dropped from 39.0 percent of the Canadian population in 2011 to 29.9 percent in 2021 (from 12,810,705 to 10,880,360); the United Church dropped from 6.1 percent to 3.3 percent (from 2,007,610 to 1,214,185); Anglicans dropped from 5.0 percent to 3.1 percent (from 1,631,845 to 1,134,315); Lutherans dropped from 1.5 percent to 0.9 percent (from 478,185

---

2. Clarke and Macdonald, *Leaving Christianity*, 11. Scholars have routinely acknowledged this significant change, but they have been unable to agree on how best to interpret it. E.g., Thiessen, *The Meaning of Sunday* and Bibby, *Resilient Gods*.

to 328,045); Presbyterians dropped from 1.4 percent to 0.8 percent (from 472,385 to 301,400); Baptists dropped from 1.9 percent to 1.2 percent (from 635,840 to 436,940); and Pentecostals dropped from 1.5 percent to 1.1 percent (from 478,705 to 399,025). Perhaps the biggest loss here is in the United Church of Canada, which lost nearly half its members. Among the most significant exceptions to this decline was Christian Orthodox, which saw a modest increase in numbers consistent with the rate of growth of the population (from 550,690 to 623,010; 1.7 percent of the population each year).

Perhaps worth noting, of course, is that the decline in Christian affiliation was not the same in every part of the country. Newfoundland showed the highest percentage of Christian affiliation with 82.4 percent, followed by Nunavut with 73.5 percent, Prince Edward Island with 67.6 percent, and New Brunswick with 67.5 percent.[3] In other provinces and territories, however, the numbers tell a different story, as will be noted briefly further below.

Growth and Stability of Other Religions

A second major headline revolves around the growth and stability of non-Christian religions. Many faiths that were once considered "minority" religions have shown significant growth. Among them, the largest over the last decade were as follows: Muslims grew from 3.2 percent of the Canadian population in 2011 to 4.9 percent in 2021 (1,054,945 to 1,775,715); Hindus grew from 1.5 percent to 2.3 percent (from 497,960 to 828,195); and Sikhs grew from 1.4 percent to 2.1 percent (from 454,965 to 771,790). It is important to note that immigration has contributed to these numbers: while immigrants to Canada at the turn of the twentieth century were primarily from Western European (i.e., predominantly Christian) countries, that is no longer the case. Perhaps more interestingly, one will note that for the first time in Canadian history, Muslims now outnumber members of the United Church of

---

3. "The Canadian Census: A Rich Portrait of the Country's Religious and Ethnocultural Diversity," *The Daily*, 26 October 2022, 16. Component of Statistics Canada catalogue no. 11-001-X.

Canada. The United Church, which was once considered something of an unofficial state church, had come into being with the understanding that it could play a part in building Canada as a Christian nation.[4] The fact that it has now been supplanted numerically by Islam provides an interesting microcosm of the story of religion in Canada.

Denomination/ Tradition	2011 Census[5]	2021 Census[6]	Difference (+/-)
Total Population	32,852,320	36,328,480	3,476,160
Catholic	12,810,705	10,880,360	-1,930,345
United	2,007,610	1,214,185	-793,425
Anglican	1,631,845	1,134,315	-497,530
Lutheran	478,185	328,045	-150,140
Presbyterian	472,385	301,400	-170,985
Baptist	635,840	436,940	-198,900
Pentecostal	478,705	399,025	-79,680
Orthodox	550,690	623,010	72,320

Table 1: Changes in Christian Affiliation; Statistics from 2011 and 2021 Canadian Censuses

Other religions had a slightly different experience. Traditional (Indigenous) Spirituality grew at a rate that mirrored the population growth, and thus held steady at 0.2 percent (from 64,940 to 80,685). Buddhists and Jewish adherents showed comparable

---

4. Airhart, *A Church with the Soul of a Nation*.
5. Data from Statistics Canada, *National Household Survey* (2011).
6. Data from Statistics Canada, *Census Profile, 2021 Census of Population* (2021).

numbers from one census to the next (366,830 to 356,975; and 329,500 to 335,295, respectively), though they could not keep pace with the population growth (1.1 percent to 1.0 percent; and 1.0 percent to 0.9 percent, respectively). The point is that while some religious groups have not kept up with the growth of the population, the numbers have remained relatively stable.

Religion	2011 Census[7]	2021 Census[8]	Difference (+/-)
Islam	1,054,945	1,775,715	720,770
Hinduism	497,960	828,195	330,235
Sikhism	454,965	771,790	316,825
Indigenous Spirituality	64,940	80,685	15,745
Buddhism	366,830	356,975	-9,855
Judaism	329,500	335,295	5,795
Total Population	32,852,320	36,328,480	3,476,160

Table 2: Changes in Non-Christian Religious Affiliation; Statistics from 2011 and 2021 Canadian Censuses

Growth of the Nones

Arguably the most significant headline is the sizable growth of those who select "no religion" in the census, commonly called "nones." In 2011, the total number of nones was 7,850,605, or 23.9 percent of the Canadian population; by 2021, this number had increased to 12,577,475, or 34.6 percent of the total population. With Christian affiliation currently at 53.3 percent, it is clear that

---

7. Data from Statistics Canada, *National Household Survey* (2011).
8. Data from Statistics Canada, *Census Profile, 2021 Census of Population* (2021).

"no religion" is rapidly closing the gap.[9] In some provinces and territories, the numbers are much closer, and in the case of British Columbia and the Yukon, nones actually outnumber Christians (52.1 percent "no religion and secular perspectives" versus 34.3 percent Christian in BC; and 59.7 percent versus 35.0 percent in YT).[10]

	2011[11]	2021[12]	Difference (+/-)
Total Population	32,852,320	36,328,480	3,476,160
No Religion	7,850,605	12,577,475	4,726,870

Table 3: Changes in "No-Religion"; Statistics from 2011 and 2021 Canadian Censuses

What accounts for this change? Joel Thiessen and Sarah Wilkins-Laflamme have identified several factors. Among them, they observe that it has become less socially taboo to identify as non-religious in today's society. Additionally, for some, religion has become too politically entwined; for others, controversies in the church or negative experiences have been too much to bear. Finally, Thiessen and Wilkins-Laflamme note that in some instances, the growth in the number of nones is less the result of people leaving the church and more a result of never entering it in the first place: in many cases, there is limited exposure to religion during childhood.[13] Regardless of the cause(s), the data hints at the future of religion in Canada: the portion of the population that se-

---

9. Viewing the data another way, in an interval of time where Christian affiliation dropped 14 percent, "no religion" increased by 10.7 percent.

10. "The Canadian Census: A Rich Portrait of the Country's Religious and Ethnocultural Diversity," *The Daily*, 26 October 2022, 16. Component of Statistics Canada catalogue no. 11-001-X.

11. Data from Statistics Canada, *National Household Survey* (2011).

12. Data from Statistics Canada, *Census Profile, 2021 Census of Population* (2021).

13. The reasons listed above are all from Thiessen and Wilkins-Laflamme, *None of the Above*, 7–12.

lects "no religion" is growing and will likely continue to grow in the days ahead.

Conclusion

The purpose of this introductory essay is not to provide any ground-breaking analysis of the census data; rather, it is to provide a background for the conversation ahead. To that end, it has identified three "headlines" in Canadian religion as demonstrated in the 2021 census data: the decline of Christian affiliation, the growth and stabilization of other religions, and the growth of the so-called nones.

What does this mean for the future of Christianity in Canada? Drawing from the census data, the takeaway here may seem reasonably clear: while not yet dead, some forms of institutional Christianity in Canada are in hospice. But, contrary to the opinion of the newspaper-holding pastor noted above, the future is not all doom and gloom. Do these results mean that Christianity is facing an extinction-level threat in Canada? It is probably not likely. What it does mean, however, is that Christianity may soon take a different form as Canada moves further into post-Christendom.

The following nine essays in this edition of *Post-Christendom Studies* address this relatively uncertain future. When we invited the contributors, we gave them a prompt: what does this mean for the church moving forward? Each author has addressed this question differently and added their own thoughts. In each essay, however, it seems reasonably clear that the newspaper headlines do not always signal that "the end is nigh."

Bibliography

Airhart, Phyllis D. *A Church with the Soul of a Nation: Making and Remaking of the United Church of Canada*. Montreal and Kingston: McGill-Queen's University Press, 2014.

Bibby, Reginald W. *Resilient Gods: Being Pro-Religious, Low-Religious, or No Religious in Canada*. Vancouver: University of British Columbia Press, 2017.

Clarke, Brian and Stuart Macdonald. *Leaving Christianity: Changing Allegiances in Canada Since 1945*. Montreal and Kingston: McGill-Queen's University Press, 2017.

Statistics Canada, National Household Survey (2011). Online: www12.statcan.gc.ca.

Statistics Canada, Census Profile, 2021 Census of Population (2021). Online: www12.statcan.gc.ca.

The Daily. "The Canadian Census: A Rich Portrait of the Country's Religious and Ethnocultural Diversity." 26 October 2022, 11–16. Component of Statistics Canada catalogue no. 11-001-X.

Thiessen, Joel. *The Meaning of Sunday: The Practice of Belief in a Secular Age*. Montreal and Kingston: McGill-Queen's University Press, 2015.

Thiessen, Joel and Sarah Wilkins-Laflamme. *None of the Above: Nonreligious Identity in the US and Canada*. Regina, SK: University of Regina Press, 2020.

When the Saints Aren't Marching In: Disaffiliation, the 2021 Census, and the Cultural Zeitgeist in Canada

Sam Reimer
Crandall University, Moncton, NB, Canada

The census data show that by 2021, just over half of Canadians claim some sort of Christian affiliation, compared to two-thirds (67.3 percent) in 2011 and three-quarters (77.1 percent) in 2001.[1] Are these disaffiliates converting to other religions? No, nearly all are becoming religious "nones," or "nonverts" as Stephen Bullivant calls them.[2] The data show 34.6 percent of Canadians claim no religious affiliation as of 2021, double of what it was in 2001.[3] These numbers may even be optimistic. A recent poll shows that half of Canadians claim no religious affiliation in 2019.[4]

This decline in Christendom can also be seen in church attendance, something the census does not ask. Since at least the 1960s, church attendance declined steadily; weekly attendance has dropped from about 67 percent in 1946 to below 10 percent today.[5] Giving to churches and volunteering are down as well. Canadians are increasingly unlikely to participate in a religious institution. This trend away from churches is widespread across

---

1. "The Canadian Census: A Rich Portrait of the Country's Religious and Ethnocultural Diversity," *The Daily*, 26 October 2022, 11–16. Component of Statistics Canada catalogue no. 11-001-X.
2. Bullivant, *Nonverts*.
3. "The Canadian Census: A Rich Portrait of the Country's Religious and Ethnocultural Diversity," *The Daily*, 26 October 2022, 11–16. Component of Statistics Canada catalogue no. 11-001-X.
4. Hiemstra, "Not Christian Anymore," n.p.
5. Clarke and Macdonald, *Leaving Christianity*; and Reimer, *Caught in the Current*.

many countries, including the US, Britain, Australia, and many European countries.[6]

However, the census tells us that not all religious groups are declining in Canada. Those that are not are mainly benefiting from immigration. Other world religions—Muslims, Sikhs, Hindus—are growing mainly because of immigration. Among Christian groups, the group that is clearly growing is Orthodox Christianity, again thanks mainly to immigration. The only other growing Christian category is those who say they are "Christian," with no other specification.[7] To the best of our knowledge, this is typically an eclectic grouping, made up of both low-commitment (who affiliate as Christian but rarely practice their faith) and high-commitment (active in church attendance and prayer) Christians. Possibly this is an indication that denominational identities are weakening, as people prefer to be known as just "Christian."

It will not surprise even casual observers of religious trends that Canada is increasingly post-Christian. The question is why? I will point out two important reasons (not an exhaustive list): immigration and a changing cultural zeitgeist. I will discuss the first briefly, and the second in more detail.

Regarding immigration, by 2032, it is predicted that 100 percent our growth will be due to immigration.[8] By 2041, it is estimated that over half of Canadians will be immigrants or children of immigrants, with a much higher percentage in our major cities.[9] Demographically, the religiosity and affiliation of immigrants will be a key driver of religious growth and decline. Immigrants tend to have higher religiosity than non-immigrants,[10] so attracting immigrants to a congregation is important for both growth and vitality. Those congregations located in our big cities (Vancouver, Toronto, Montreal) have an advantage because immigrants are

6. Inglehart, *Religion's Sudden Decline*.
7. "The Canadian Census: A Rich Portrait of the Country's Religious and Ethnocultural Diversity," *The Daily*, 26 October 2022, 11–16. Component of Statistics Canada catalogue no. 11-001-X.
8. Government of Canada, "An immigration plan to grow the economy," n.p.
9. Stats Canada, "Canada in 2041," n.p.
10. Reimer and Hiemstra, "The Gains/Losses," 327–44.

still more likely to land in our big cities than elsewhere. Of course, the pre-arrival religious affiliation of immigrants will shape the future of the religious landscape in Canada. Besides Orthodox Christians, significant numbers of Catholic and Pentecostal immigrants are bolstering their numbers of affiliates. Yet, even these groups are losing ground, if not as quickly as other groups that benefit less from immigration (like the United Church or Lutherans).

If 400,000–500,000 immigrants a year cannot reverse the religious decline in Canada,[11] then what is the cause of so much disaffiliation? The typical answer from scholars is secularization; and that is a good answer. Very briefly, secularization theory would posit that religious authority is declining in Canada and other Western countries.[12] Secularization is driven by macro-structural factors like differentiation, where religious influences are removed from other major institutions like schools, politics, economy, media, and health care. As a result, people's public life lacks religious significance, and religion is sequestered to the private sphere of our homes and our weekend activities (privatization). Pluralization is another factor. As our society becomes more religiously diverse, no one religious view has taken-for-granted legitimacy. Berger's *Sacred Canopy* (1967) has been replaced by individual umbrellas.[13] Further, scientific explanations have replaced religious explanations for many things, and modernization and technological advances provide a comfortable (and distracted!) life such that the desire for religious compensators (i.e., rewards in heaven for present suffering) is muted.

Yet, these macro social changes are not the whole story. As I argue in my recent book, cultural factors are also in play.[14] Put succinctly, our dominant culture narrative, the cultural *Zeitgeist*, is pushing us away from institutional religion.

---

11. Government of Canada, "An immigration plan to grow the economy," n.p.
12. Chaves, "Secularization as Declining Religious Authority," 749–74.
13. Carwana, "Evangelicals." See also Berger, *The Sacred Canopy*.
14. Reimer, *Caught in the Current*.

Firstly, this is because deference to institutional authorities like politicians, parents, teachers, clergy, and medical doctors is on the decline, while deference to our own intuition is increasing. Authority has moved from outside the person to inside the person. Eminent philosopher Charles Taylor calls this "the massive subjective turn in modern culture."[15] We are expected to follow the dictates of our own hearts instead of the blindly following the dictates of some religious authority. Canadians are increasingly guided by an inner epistemology.[16] We are told that we are our own source of truth. Society prescribes "following our own path" or "being true to yourself." Ironically, the authority of social media and the internet, called "algorithmic authority" by Heidi Campbell,[17] seems immune to critique, and Canadians do not seem to realize that this external authority is (mis)shaping them.

As a result of this shift to an inner locus of authority, Canadians feel free to disagree with the official doctrines of a denomination if it does not resonate with what they sense within. "Sure," a Canadian may think, "we can make use of a church for a time if it helps us on our individual journey toward wholeness, but we feel no sense of loyalty because we have to find our own path." I suggest that this shift toward inner authority is the greatest barrier to Christian discipleship in our society. It is hard to pass on the faith to the next generation if everyone has to discover their beliefs (and even their identity) for themselves.

Secondly, "religion" (the word itself) has negative connotations for many in Canadian society.[18] For example, the abuses associated with the indigenous residential schools, including the purported discovery of mass graves, have changed the perception of religion. Religion, especially Christianity, actively participated in this abuse and the suppression of indigenous religion and culture. As a result, religious authority is associated with "colonialism" and "oppression" for many. Another example would be the association of religion with what is happening south of the border.

15. Taylor, *The Ethics of Authenticity*, 26.
16. Watts, *The Spiritual Turn*.
17. Campbell, *Digital Creatives*.
18. Watts and Reimer, "Symbolic Pollution and Religious Change," n.p.

The role of Christianity in American nationalism, kindled by the rhetoric of former President Trump and some conservative religious leaders, has fed this association. "Religion" is symbolically linked with "American." Since Canadian identity is partly a negative identity (that is, we are not Americans), religion, especially conservative and committed religion, is seen as "un-Canadian." I could also mention the scandals of religious leaders, which link religion to hypocrisy and greed in the minds of some.

Overall, the point is that the macrostructural changes normally associated with secularization are not the whole story. Cultural changes, like the shift to internal authority and the increasingly negative connotation of religion, also play a role. These changes are symbolic and cultural, and affect people's feelings toward religion, which also influence their participation in it. The census reveals the surface symptoms of a massive, subterranean cultural shift.

This sounds like mostly bad news for Christian ministry. If clergy are only interested in big churches and full pews, then it is bad news. Clearly, attracting Canadians to church is a tough task if they view institutional Christianity negatively. A more herculean task, I would argue, is to teach Canadians to defer to the external authority of God and the Bible, when the cultural script instructs them to follow the inner directives of their heart.

However, one can also argue that the cultural scaffolding that supported Christianity, and artificially props up church participation, is now gone. This means that people participate in congregations less for conventional reasons and more for reasons of commitment. Possibly the disaffiliation of marginal members, leaving only a committed core, is good for Christianity. As our British co-religionists are learning, Christianity can thrive in the margins of society.[19]

Bibliography

Berger, Peter. *The Sacred Canopy: Elements of a Sociological Theory of Religion.* New York: Anchor, 1967.

---

19. Webster, "2021 Census," n.p.

Bullivant, Stephen. *Nonverts: The Making of Ex-Christian America*. Oxford: Oxford University Press, 2022.

Campbell, Heidi. *Digital Creatives and the Rethinking of Religious Authority*. London: Routledge, 2020.

Carwana, Brian. "Evangelicals, the Liberal State, and Canada's Family Values Debates: The Struggle to Shape Selves." PhD diss., University of Toronto, 2021.

Chaves, Mark. "Secularization as Declining Religious Authority." *Social Forces* 72 (1994) 749–74.

Government of Canada. 2022. "An immigration plan to grow the economy." N.p. online: https://www.canada.ca/en/immigration-refugees-citizenship/news/2022/11/an-immigration-plan-to-grow-the-economy.html.

Hiemstra, Rick. "Not Christian Anymore." *Faith Today*, January/February 2020. N.p. online: https://www.faithtoday.ca/Magazines/2020-Jan-Feb/Not-Christian-anymore.

The Daily. "The Canadian Census: A Rich Portrait of the Country's Religious and Ethnocultural Diversity," 26 October 2022, 11–16. Component of Statistics Canada catalogue no. 11-001-X.

Inglehart, Ronald. *Religion's Sudden Decline: What's Causing It, and What Comes Next?* Oxford: Oxford University Press, 2021.

Reimer, Sam. *Caught in the Current: British and Canadian Evangelicals in an Age of Self-Spirituality*. Montreal and Kingston: McGill-Queen's University Press, 2023.

Reimer, Sam and Rick Hiemstra. "The Gains/Losses of Canadian Religious Groups from Immigration: Immigration Flows, Attendance and Switching." *Studies in Religion* 47 (2018) 327–44.

Stats Canada. "Canada in 2041: A larger, more diverse population with greater differences between regions," 2022. N.p. online: https://www150.statcan.gc.ca/n1/daily-quotidien/220908/dq220908a-eng.htm.

Taylor, Charles. *The Ethics of Authenticity*. Cambridge, MA: Harvard University Press, 1991.

Watts, Galen. *The Spiritual Turn: The Religion of the Heart and the Making of Romantic Liberal Modernity*. Oxford: Oxford University Press, 2022.

Watts, Galen and Sam Reimer. "Symbolic Pollution and Religious Change: The Religious Imaginary of Anglo-Canadian *Spiritual but not Religious* Millennials." *Sociology of Religion*, in press.

Webster, Danny. "2021 Census: Christianity can Flourish in the Margins of Society," 2022. N.p. online: https://www.eauk.org/news-and-views/census-figures-we-are-not-surprised-but-there-is-work-to-do.

More Buddhists than Baptists?:
A Call to Reframe Baptist Discourse
for Mission in Canada

Anna Robbins
Acadia Divinity College, Wolfville, NS, Canada

Living in a region where Baptist heritage looms large, it is interesting to note that there are almost as many Buddhists as Baptists in Canada today. We should not be surprised. Nationally, the number of people of the Baptist faith has never been significant, though their concentration differs in various regions of the country. Still, along with most other Christian families, the Baptists have watched their numbers decline steadily, while the numbers of Buddhists have continued to increase at the same rate. Indeed, the number of Buddhists in British Columbia and Ontario outnumber Baptists, though each religious group only forms merely one to two percent of the population nationally.

When compared with the growth of other religions, this reality is even more notable. There are twice as many Hindus as Baptists and three times as many Muslims. Yet, there are some Baptists alarmed to find a Musjid being built in their town where there are at least 20 Baptist Churches within a few kilometers. Many of these churches sit on the perilous brink of existence, looking down at those who have already gone over and wondering how long they might hang on.

Baptists perhaps often overestimated their strength and numbers, as have Christians overall. I remember forty years ago in school and later university being one of very few people of faith, a reality we simply accepted. In primary school days, we had Bible reading and prayer to start the day and said the Lord's Prayer in senior school assembly. Christianity in this form was simply latent in culture, and the only person who seemed to take faith seriously was the Chemistry teacher, who was hysterical when she found out there was someone coming to speak at the school offering a "scientific" calculation of how Noah fit all of the world's animal species in the ark.

When my husband and I were first dating, he was the only person on our large residence floor who would come to church with me. He had not yet come to faith, and there was only one other person besides me who identified as Christian. When he told his family he was being baptized by immersion, they were concerned he was joining a cult. I knew through my educational experience that Christians were few, but that was the first time I realized how odd it was to be a Baptist.

The reality is that the story of the decline into ever smaller numbers in the 2021 census should surprise no one. Canada has diversified. The number of Christians is declining, and the Baptists along with them. As a new generation of Canadian-born people distance themselves ever further from their inherited faith traditions, immigrants are reported to be far more religiously committed. A majority of immigrants to Canada still identify as Christian. This no doubt bolsters the numbers in churches on Sunday while the next generation of Canadian-born Christians is eroding.[1]

As others have noted, immigrants bring with them deep religious commitment, Christian and otherwise, that impacts our public religious landscape. Johanna Lewis has noted that religiously committed immigrants come with an expectation that their religion will have an impact on the public sphere.[2] This may concern those who have developed over time a largely quietist attitude to faith in the public realm, but it may also bring encouragement to acknowledge that no faith can be entirely private.

All of this affirms a trajectory of change that sees Christians in general—and groups like Baptists in particular—in an increasingly marginalized position in Canadian culture. As they contemplate the demographic shifts in Canadian society, are Baptists able to

---

1. Sam Reimer and Rick Hiemstra ("The Gains/Losses," 327–44) noted before the most recent census that immigrants bolster number of all religions in Canada, including Christianity.
2. Lewis, "Religion and Belief," n.p.

reimagine their identity and shape their discourse in a way that converges with a new vision of Canada, or are we relegated to polarization and marginalization by our own design? Are Baptist leaders able to engage the mission of the church in society with transformative action that is faithfully distinctive and yet winsome and nurturing of diverse cultures? Or will they be keepers of ever smaller aquariums until there are no fish left inside?

As Gordon Heath has suggested, there are moments in history where changing discourse sets the trajectory of Baptist life in Canada.[3] He notes that the discourse that surrounds these moments has shown Baptists to be adaptable to significant change in the interests of mission. For example, in the decline of empire, Baptists were able to reimagine their identity away from Anglo-Saxon exclusivity, suggesting a new trajectory for Baptist life that stretches to the present. Most importantly, he indicates, "What is noteworthy is that in the midst of tumultuous and terrifying times, much of the discourse of the churches facilitated rather than bucked that reimagining of the nation."[4]

Just as Baptists in the past have shaped the discourse for mission in a changing cultural context, it would seem advisable to rediscover their identity in a missional calling today. Declining numbers and influence leave Baptists across the country reacting to their increased insignificance by marginalizing themselves in their response to culture and polarizing within the ranks. At a time when Baptist distinctives could provide a common center for Baptist identity in Canada, mission is jettisoned for culture wars and sectarianism.

There is a temptation amongst many today to form a collective identity by naming a common enemy. Carl Schmidt, the political theologian of Germany's Third Reich, seems to be everywhere. Schmidt insisted that a group comes to know who they are by identifying their shared enemy. Internationally and within national borders, the identification of a common enemy is a widespread

---

3. Heath, "Canadian Baptists and the Fall(ing) of the British Empire," n.p.
4. Heath, "Canadian Baptists and the Fall(ing) of the British Empire," n.p.

practice. In Canada, there is a polarizing left and right that has a menacing feel because it is not only predicated on difference but also the idea that those who are different are dangerous.

In a country that posits diversity as its greatest strength, Canadians may be struggling to live into diversity when internet algorithms and nefarious forces are interfering to create division. Baptists and other Christians become subject to the same forces of suspicion. Instead of finding common identity in the Lordship of Christ, it is found in defining the enemy. The enemy used to be out there somewhere, but now, the enemy is within and needs to be called out.

And so, we see Baptists across the country falling out over views on cultural engagement without recognizing that the culture they live in has raised an entire generation of young people with an open view on sexuality, gender, and a host of other issues. To draw hard lines now on such issues alienates an entire culture whose people cannot understand the attitudes of exclusion they face. At the same time, some immigrant communities may hold to a hardline on these similar issues. Yet, rather than frame cultural engagement as mission, culture is often regarded as a common enemy. In a culture war brought inside the walls of the church, both sides become entrenched, believing that the other is the unbiblical compromiser of truth. The divide becomes ever greater.

Can Baptists expect to survive such division when there are so many other factors that mitigate against a thriving Christian faith? If the discourse is shaped solely as a matter of dogma, polarization increases to the point of fragmentation, as Baptists across Canada have experienced in discussions around sexuality. Views are called out as unbiblical by both sides, and accusations of gospel compromise are universally made. Baptists face the danger of fragmenting into oblivion so long as the discourse is shaped around doctrinal ethics without referencing mission.

If Baptists were to take their mission seriously today, they might ask questions about how a gospel presentation could be offered in a way that could be heard and understood in Canadian culture today.⁵ Is cohesion of Baptist life possible in Canada now? Can Baptists live into their mission fully if they fail to stick together? Can Baptists, and indeed Christians, learn to engage the public realm winsomely from the position of numerical and practical marginalization? How might internal and external Baptist discourse contribute to the direction of Canadian diversity rather than resist it?

Perhaps some guidance exists within Baptist distinctives themselves. The Baptist distinctive of the Lordship of Christ, for example, humbles perspectives and relativizes extremes when it is recognized that Jesus is above all views and perspectives. The fact of Christ's Lordship holds Baptists in unity even when they differ on some aspects of how that is lived out. The Lordship of Christ calls us to humility regarding our theological views that are by necessity tentative unless we think ourselves immune to the noetic effects of sin.

The Lordship of Christ beckons us to recognize the competency of each soul to decide for themselves how to serve God and that the mind of Christ is discerned in the meeting of each congregation. That has never yielded unanimity in practice but calls us to respect the dignity of others' spirituality. Moreover, soul competency spills over into the advocacy for freedom of each to believe and worship however they wish, something Baptist forebears in the faith have died for, arguing that whether Muslim, Buddhist, Hindu, or atheist, no one should be compelled to religious belief. Baptists could have a unique role to play in defending the religious freedom of all in Canada, creating a discourse that shapes the diversity of Canada in ways that are inclusive of all, including Christians. Rooting identity in Baptist distinctives rather than in some perceived common enemy produces a missional discourse worth pursuing.

As churches continue to decline, unity rather than fragmentation suggests a potentially flourishing future. Beyond the dis-

---

5. Tillich, *Theology of Culture*. In this classic work, Tillich identifies the pre-apologetic task, which is to engage in a correlative process to be able to prepare a culture to receive a Christian message that is so alien as to be incomprehensible.

agreements within, Baptists may be able to find ways to reach out to other Christians and work for the common good together with those of other religions out of respect for universal human dignity and soul competency. Baptists might then develop a discourse that regards increasing religious diversity as a positive cultural reality for Christians in Canada and recapture a sense of mission to culture that draws circles around people rather than lines between them.

Bibliography

Heath, Gordon L. "Canadian Baptists and the Fall(ing) of the British Empire, 1945–1956." George Rawlyk Memorial Lecture in Baptist Studies, Acadia Divinity College, Acadia University, 20 September 2022.

Lewis, Johanna. "Religion and Belief Among Immigrants to Canada." *Cardus Research Brief* (July 2023) n.p. Online: https://www.cardus.ca/research/faith-communities/research-brief/religion-and-belief-among-immigrants-to-canada.

Reimer, Sam and Rick Hiemstra. "The Gains/Losses of Canadian Religious Groups from Immigration: Immigration Flows, Attendance and Switching." *Studies in Religion/Sciences Religieuses* 47:3 (2018–2019) 327–44.

Tillich, Paul. *Theology of Culture*. Oxford: Oxford University Press, 1959.

Through a Clear Window: The 2021 Census Helps us See Christianity in Canada Today

Stuart Macdonald
Knox College, Toronto, ON, Canada

It is not because of the pandemic. You might think it is, and that is understandable. The COVID-19 pandemic has certainly made it challenging for many congregations. Congregational life was severely disrupted by the abrupt need to cease in-person worship in March 2020. What we imagined might be for a few weeks ended up being for much, much longer. There was no one moment where we could all declare our churches "open." There was a long, confusing process with changing requirements along the way, different comfort levels for attending (both by ministers, priests and pastors, and members of the congregation), and false starts as new variants forced renewed restrictions to be imposed. After a turbulent period, congregations are back to in-person worship. But things are not the same. Anecdotally, I have heard of many situations where congregational attendance is only gradually coming back to what it was prior to March 2020. Some people seem quite happy to continue to worship remotely rather than in-person. The impact on the number of children present in worship seems particularly striking. Minister colleagues who reported having some children present each Sunday before March 2020 now note that on most Sundays, it is simply adults. Clearly, the pandemic had an impact. One can argue that it has sped up the challenges congregations were already facing. But—and this is important to pause and remember—it did not create those changes. The larger demographic shifts were well underway before the pandemic hit. The number of congregations deciding they are no longer financially viable may have been accelerated by the pandemic; the root causes have been there for years. We may now be experiencing a tipping point in congregational viability. But, the roots of this go back decades.

The dramatic changes in the place of Christianity within Canada were made clear when the results of the 2021 census were published in October 2022. The Statistics Canada report, "The Canadian Census: A Rich Portrait of the Country's Religious and Ethnocultural Diversity," focused, as the title suggested, on the ethnic, cultural, racial and religious diversity of Canada. Religion was one of the major subheadings: "Religion: another facet of diversity in Canada."[1] Christians, the report noted, remained the largest religious group in Canada. This remained true even though these numbers were decreasing, while the numbers of those of other religious traditions were increasing.[2] Those who reported that they had "no religious affiliation" or a "secular perspective (atheist, agnostic, humanist and other secular perspectives)" was the other group that experienced dramatic growth.[3] Indeed, those Canadians with no religious affiliation now represented 34.6 percent of the population, up from 23.9 percent a decade previously in 2011, and 16.5 percent the decade before that 2001.[4] The other data that emerged from the 2021 census confirmed this picture that long-term trends were continuing. Another publication of Statistics Canada released earlier in the year, "The impact of the COVID-19 Pandemic on the Religiosity of Canadians," confirmed that, while the pandemic had a clear impact on religious groups in

---

1. "The Canadian Census: A Rich Portrait of the Country's Religious and Ethnocultural Diversity," *The Daily*, 26 October 2022, 11–16. Component of Statistics Canada catalogue no. 11-001-X.
2. "The Canadian Census: A Rich Portrait of the Country's Religious and Ethnocultural Diversity," *The Daily*, 26 October 2022, 12. Component of Statistics Canada catalogue no. 11-001-X.
3. "The Canadian Census: A Rich Portrait of the Country's Religious and Ethnocultural Diversity," *The Daily*, 26 October 2022, 13. Component of Statistics Canada catalogue no. 11-001-X.
4. "The Canadian Census: A Rich Portrait of the Country's Religious and Ethnocultural Diversity," *The Daily*, 26 October 2022, 13. Component of Statistics Canada catalogue no. 11-001-X.

Canada, that impact was limited.[5] Put directly, the pandemic had an impact: but the trends already in place largely continued. There was, as one of the subheadings noted "no visible effect of the pandemic on religious affiliation trends."[6]

The data published in the report on the 2021 census confirmed what scholars had already been noting about the changing place of Christianity in Canada. As one of the co-authors of *Leaving Christianity: Changing Allegiances in Canada since 1945*, it was interesting to see how new data reinforced many of the conclusions we had reached. The picture has become even clearer. Those claiming "no religion" are here to stay and a significant feature of the Canadian religious landscape. In contrast, every recognizable major Christian religious tradition in the country, with only one exception, has seen a decline in the number in the number of Canadians affiliated with that tradition. (See Table 1).[7] Overall those who identified as Christians declined from 22.1 million to 19.3 million (or -12 percent). That decline was reflected across the various Christian traditions from the United Church (-40 percent) to the Pentecostals (-17 percent), from the Baptists (-31 percent) to the Lutherans (-31 percent), and included the Latter Day Saints (-50 percent), the Anglicans (-30 percent), and the Presbyterians (-36 percent). The only identifiable tradition which experienced growth was the Orthodox who saw their numbers grow by about 75,000 or 13 percent. Immigration, one can reasonably assume, is a major factor in this growth. Finally, the Canadians who simply

---

5. Lacasse and Cornelissen, "The impact of the COVID-19." This report gives excellent information on the particular impacts of the pandemic on practice and other issues.

6. Lacasse and Cornelissen, "The impact of the COVID-19," 8.

7. Statistics Canada, Table 98-10-0343-01 "Religion by immigrant status and period of immigration and place of birth: Canada, provinces and territories," Released 2022-10-26, was used in this analysis. Table 98-10-0342-01, "Religion by visible minority and generation status: Canada, provinces and territories, census metropolitan areas and census agglomerations with parts," Released 2022-10-26, gives further detail on the smaller traditions which make up some of these larger traditions (for example, the Canadian Reformed Church and the Christian Reformed Church are two of the traditions within the broader category of Reformed). The current paper focused on the main categories and those groups which could be compared to the 2011 census data.

told the census they were "Christian" (with no further qualification or identified denomination) exploded—again. This group, which was about 1.5 million strong in 2011, is now approximately 2.7 million strong, a growth rate of 87 percent. More research on this group is needed and will undoubtedly take place. In the meantime, caution should be exercised. Our research on the census to 2011 discovered that this was a far more complex and diverse group than is often assumed.[8] It is also worth remembering that, despite this group's growth, the overall number of those who identified as Christians in Canada nevertheless declined by over 2.7 million affiliates.

The change over the last twenty years is dramatic. The Statistics Canada report on the religious data in the 2021 census provides evidence of some striking changes. At the same time, this twenty-year time frame is simply inadequate if we want to truly understand and appreciate how dramatic a change this really represents. As reported in the census, those Canadians with no religious affiliation now stand at 35 percent of the population, more than double what was reported twenty years ago. Yet, what we really need to understand and appreciate was that this figure was consistently below 1 percent of the Canadian population up to and including the 1961 census. Even when the census changed from being done by personal interviews to being anonymous in 1971, that number had only grown to 4 percent. To understand the dramatic shift in religiosity in Canada, comparisons are needed to the time when Christian affiliation was strong in Canada—in particular, the 1950s and early 1960s. The change over the last sixty years becomes even more apparent when we consider a longer time scale.

---

8. Clarke and Macdonald, *Leaving Christianity*.

Denomination/Tradition	2011	2021	% Growth/decline
Catholic	12810710	10880360	-15%
Christian Orthodox	550965	623005	**13%**
United Church	2007615	1214185	-40%
Anglican Church	1631845	1134310	-30%
Presbyterian	473380	301400	-36%
Lutheran	478185	328045	-31%
Baptist	635840	436940	-31%
Pentecostal and other charismatic	478705	399030	-17%
Jehovah's Witness	137775	137255	0%
Latter Day Saints	175880	87725	-50%
Reformed	102825	79870	-22%
Christian (not otherwise specified)	1475575	2760755	**87%**
Christian	22102480	19373330	-12%
no religion	7850610	12577475	**60%**

Table 1: Percentage change of selected Christian traditions, Christians, and no religious affiliation—2011 and 2021. Source: 2021 census data Table 98-10-0343-01, released 2022-10-26; 2011 census.

Christians in Canada have become a much smaller percentage of the overall population. In some traditions, they have also become much older. What is striking in the data provided in the 2021 census is how much younger those without a religious affiliation are. As Figure 1 shows, the percentage of those with no religion in the younger cohorts (under 44) exceed the percentage of the total population in these cohorts. Put simply, those with no religion are younger. This is not news but is further confirmation of this trend.[9] In contrast, Canadians who have a Christian identity seem to skew older. This is clearly the case in terms of the United Church of Canada (Figure 2). The United Church has few affiliates in the cohorts below 35–44. The percentage of the United Church affiliates in each of these cohorts is strikingly less than what one finds within the total Canadian population. This continues to be true, though not as dramatically, in the 45–54 age cohort. Indeed, it is clear that the majority of United Church affiliates are over 55, dramatically more as a percentage of the institution than is the case for the total population in Canada. The 2021 census dramatically confirms what many have observed about who is in the pews of this denomination's congregations. But it is important to recognize that it has not always been this way. As Brian Clarke and I demonstrated in *Leaving Christianity*, in 1961 the United Church of Canada's census affiliates fit very closely the age profile of the Canadian population. There were the same percentage of young people in the United Church as there were in the population.[10] We also noted that this had changed by 2001, with United Church affiliates being significantly older.[11] What the data from 2021 does is confirm that this trend is continuing, even intensifying. What this also confirms, then, is that what we are witnessing in at least some Christian traditions is generationally driven change. Those who were affiliates of the United Church of Canada in 1961 have not left, they have simply become older. Younger Canadians, including those baptized in the United Church, failed to become life-long affiliates of that denomination. Note again that this began more than twenty years ago. Indeed, data suggests that this rupture happened—for whatever reason or series of reasons—in the mid-1960s.[12] Is the United Church unique in this re-

---

9. Clarke and Macdonald, *Leaving Christianity*, 169–73.
10. Clarke and Macdonald, *Leaving Christianity*, 38 (Figure 1.1).
11. Clarke and Macdonald, *Leaving Christianity*, 39 (Figure 1.2). The discussion is on pp. 37–38.
12. Clarke and Macdonald, *Leaving Christianity*, 53–55, 197–231. Flatt, *After Evangelicalism*.

gard? Or is it merely an example of this trend, one that other denominations or traditions might want to consider, not merely anecdotally, but using the data available through the census?

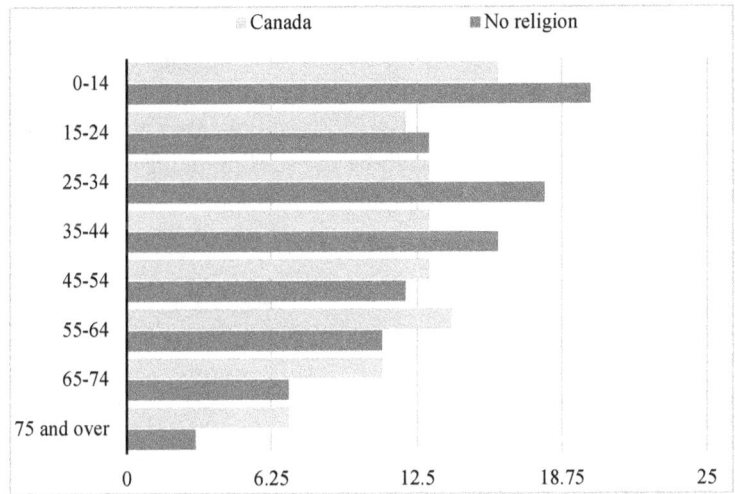

Figure 1: Percentage of Canadian population, and those indicating no religion, in age cohorts in 2021 census. Source: 2021 census data Table 98-10-0343-01, released 2022-10-26.

Data from the 2021 census brings into even sharper focus the changed place of the Christian tradition in Canada. The pandemic may have accelerated the situation, but the trends have been developing over decades. Canada is different, not only from what it was twenty years ago but even more so from the early post-WWII era that saw a religious revival and expansion of Christian affiliations, memberships, and institutions. That Canada is long gone. While we may gain insights from further research—for example into the age profiles of specific denominations, or a better understanding of who exactly is in the category of "Christian" in the census—the broad picture is clear. We are a post-Christendom, post-Christian country. Similar trends seem to be emerging in the United States. While it will be interesting to learn more about "The Great Dechurching," to use the phrase Jim Davis and Michael Graham have applied to the American situation, Canadians should be cautious in assuming that this reflects our experience.[13] The growth of those stating they had "no religion" started earlier in Canada and seems much more entrenched. Canadians need to focus on the excellent work that has been done over the last decade on religious change in this country, including suggestions of how we need to respond to this change. It is time to stop denying and start adapting. I am deeply appreciative of Lee Beach's *The Church in Exile: Living in Hope After Christendom*.[14] This book takes our changed situation seriously. This needs to be the starting point for congregations and denominations: taking the situation seriously and moving forward in faith.

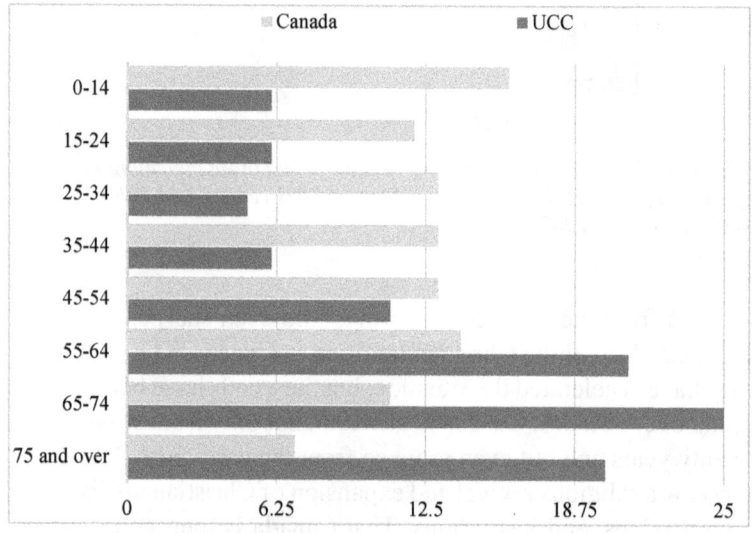

Figure 2: Percentage of Canadian population, and those indicating United Church of Canada (UCC), in age cohorts in 2021 census. Source: 2021 census data Table 98-10-0343-01, released 2022-10-26.

13. Davis et al., *The Great Dechurching*.
14. Beach, *The Church in Exile*.

Trying to move back to what is remembered as a golden age (which, indeed, may have existed) is not helpful. Nor is it possible. The 2021 census data on religion confirms that we are in a vastly different Canada. It is time to accept this and move forward.

Bibliography

Beach, Lee. *The Church in Exile: Living in Hope After Christendom*. Downers Grove: IVP Academic, 2015.

Clarke, Brian, and Stuart Macdonald. *Leaving Christianity: Changing Allegiances in Canada since 1945*. Montreal and Kingston: McGill-Queens University Press, 2017.

Davis, Jim, et al. *The Great Dechurching: Who's Leaving, Why Are They Going, and What Will It Take to Bring Them Back?* Grand Rapids: Zondervan, 2023.

Flatt, Kevin. *After Evangelicalism: The Sixties and the United Church of Canada*. Montreal and Kingston: McGill-Queen's University Press, 2013.

Lacasse, Simon-Pierre, and Louis Cornelissen. "The Impact of the COVID-19 Pandemic on the Religiosity of Canadians." Statistics Canada, 18 July 2022.

The Daily. "The Canadian Census: A Rich Portrait of the Country's Religious and Ethnocultural Diversity." 26 October 2022, 11–16. Component of Statistics Canada catalogue no. 11-001-X.

HAPPY IS THE LAND THAT ROBS FROM GOD: SECULARIZING CANADA IN THE MID-NINETEENTH CENTURY

James Tyler Robertson
Tyndale University, Toronto, ON, Canada

"Institutions do not protect themselves. They fall one after the other, unless each is defended from the beginning. So choose an institution you care about . . . And take its side."[1]

Introduction

Statistics Canada's 2021 census findings caused concern for many churches across the nation. Trends seem to indicate that Canadians, more than ever before, possess "no religious affiliation."[2] While such statements lack nuance and do not communicate the full story of Canadian religion, leaders are searching for tools to navigate the "shifting landscape of Canadian religion."[3] The contribution of this article is to offer an example from Canadian history that states simply: Canada has been here before.

In 1850, the Anglican Archdeacon of York, Andrew Bethune, stated ruefully, "When this spoliation shall be rendered complete, there may Sir, be a class who will pronounce this a really free and happy country!"[4] For him, the spoliation of Canada was not a shifting landscape of religious opinion but the issue of Clergy Re-

---

1. Snyder, *On Tyranny*, 22.
2. Thompson, "More Canadians," n.p. Another useful article is Cornelissen, "Religiosity in Canada," n.p.
3. See the Cardus study authored by Pennings and Los, "The Shifting Landscape of Faith in Canada," n.p. In it, the authors note their paper comes from a Spring 2022 panel with nine groups of religious leaders desiring to "start an ongoing dialogue about how to navigate a rapidly shifting spiritual landscape in Canada."
4. Bethune, *The Clergy Reserve Question*, 16.

serves. The Reserves comprised roughly one-seventh of colonial lands set apart by the Imperial Government to build churches and, through sales or rental revenue, financially support Church of England and Church of Scotland clergy for the spiritual edification of colonists.[5] Popular opinion held that revenues generated should be used for the betterment of all Canadians rather than the advancement of a couple of denominations.[6] For Bethune and others like him, those who supported such a stance were not simply undermining a historic British institution but were in open rebellion against God. Though the whims of the age leaned towards removing the Reserves from their clerical role, Bethune reminded Canadians that "in sober afterthoughts," they would come to recognize no "country is to be congratulated where the Church of God has been robbed."[7]

---

5. Church of Scotland claims to the Reserves was a long and drawn-out battle between them and Church of England leadership; the latter believing they were to be the sole beneficiaries. There is not sufficient space in this article to delve into that. Suffice it to say that, by 1824, the Church of Scotland qualified as a Protestant established church and was, therefore, granted access to Reserves funds. This formed a legal precedent utilized by the other denominations to finally convince the Government to dismantle the Reserves in order to honor the religiously diverse landscape of Upper and Lower Canada.

6. As is seen in one line from this Petition to the King (Various Authors, "Petition to the Provincial Parliament," 1), the Reserves were viewed as oppressive to "a very large majority of the people of this Province are now suffering, and for a long series of years have, suffered, positive although indirect persecution on account of their religious opinions."

7. "There will not, surely, be many who, in sober afterthoughts, will heartily respond to that sentiment,—that a country is to be congratulated where the Church of God has been robbed." Bethune, *The Clergy Reserve Question*, 12. He would go on to note that, given the largely agrarian nature of the economy, colonists were flirting with ruin if they continued to entertain the notion of disbanding the Reserves. Bethune wrote: "Can we, in such a condition of rebellion against the Most High, hope for bountiful harvests and commercial success,—credit abroad, or trustfulness amongst ourselves? With such dishonour to Almighty God, sanctioned by the public voice . . . can the country prosper? Not, if we are to believe in the immutability of the plans and purposes of the Divine Providence. 'Ye are cursed with a curse; for ye have robbed me, even this whole nation.'" Bethune, *The Clergy Reserve Question*, 16.

Whether we are talking about declining religious allegiances in the twenty-first century or the Clergy Reserves question of the nineteenth, the true concern seems to be the damage wrought upon society when trusted religious institutions are abandoned. Without such institutions, will the citizenry take their faith seriously? What would religion even look like if people could choose whatever belief system strikes their fancy? What will happen to social conscience? What will happen to social order? If faith has no discipline, how long until the entire nation descends into vice? This reflection explores the nineteenth-century issue of secularizing the Clergy Reserves as analogous to the issues around declining institutional Christianity today.[8]

Societal Need for Clergy Reserves

Institutions, be they religious or non, offer community and safeguard people from their selfish desires. In the words of George Chalmers: "the spontaneous demand of human beings for religion is far short of the actual interest which they have in it . . . the less we have of it, the less we desire it."[9] As beneficiaries of funds from the Reserves, it is easy to dismiss the chastisements of men like Bethune and Chalmers as unduly influenced by personal interest. However, we are better served if we take seriously concerns

---

8. This was also a time when many of the so-called norms of Canadian faith were established as it pertained to denominational loyalty. Returning to the Cardus article: "Canada's religious landscape remained largely unchanged from the mid-nineteenth century until the end of World War II, when the majority of Canadians identified as Roman Catholic or Protestant."

9. Quoting George Chalmers: "the spontaneous demand of human beings for religion is far short of the actual interest which they have in it. This is not so with their demand for food or raiment, or any article which ministers to the necessities of our physical nature. The more destitute we are of these articles the greater is our desire after them. But the case is widely different when the appetite for any good is short of that degree in which that good is useful or necessary; and above all, when just in proportion to our want of it, is the decay of our appetite towards it. Now this is, generally speaking, the case with religious instruction, the less we have of it, the less we desire it." Bethune, *The Clergy Reserve Question*, 15.

from clergy that the demise of the Reserves could also signal the demise of Canadian Christianity.

Throughout the 1820s, Reverend John Strachan of York composed several narratives, complete with dubious statistics, to support the claim that most Canadians were disposed to become Anglican if only the church could secure greater funds to support staff.[10] For Strachan, the Anglican Church was necessary to inculcate loyalty to the disparate collection of colonists who comprised the Canadas and the Maritimes. More than the government or the sparse social organizations present in the colony, the church stood above them all as the institution best suited to "infuse into the inhabitants a tone and feeling entirely English."[11]

For Bethune, "Britain has grown great under [this] present system," especially in comparison to America. Britain's constitution proved the Empire was "pre-eminently a religious nation, she has become so . . . through the influence of her Established Church."[12] The perpetual threat of America's anti-establishment ideologies creeping north had been undergirding Anglican concerns since the conclusion of the Revolutionary War in the eighteenth century.

In 1786, the Rev. John Stuart feared his inability to routinely contact Loyalist settlements around his base at Cataraqui opened space for rival churches. His letter to the Society for the Propagation of the Gospel (SPG) could offer only generalities about the religious proclivities of the outer settlements. He felt confident to

---

10. There is insufficient space in this article to offer a comprehensive overview of the Clergy Reserves question. For the sake of this reflection, it will suffice to state that from 1820–1850 colonial officials in the metropolis of London were vexed by managing these lands. The Clergy Reserves were part of the larger British belief that an established church was essential for a society to maintain Christian character. For more on this see Moir, *Church and the State*.

11. "Two or three hundred Clergymen living in Upper Canada, in the midst of their Congregations, and receiving the greater portion of their income from funds deposited in the Mother Country, must attach still more intimately the population of the Colony to the Parent State. Their influence would gradually spread, and they would infuse into the inhabitants a tone and feeling entirely English; so that the very first sentiments and opinions of the youth must become British." Strachan, *A Speech*, 7.

12. Bethune, *The Clergy Reserve Question*, 5.

write only, "they seem well disposed to attend divine Service, and show no aversion to the discipline and principles of the Church of England"[13] Stuart's report also addressed concerns that republicanism could infect even ardent Loyalists and saw any balking of Anglican discipline as indicative of American stubbornness within the people.

Combatting Rival Ideologies

Returning to Rev. John Strachan, the insidious and ubiquitous presence of Episcopal (American) Methodists, Baptists, Congregationalists, and other more "enthusiastic" versions of the faith were the greatest threats to the soul of the colony. The crux of his concerns was their ongoing connection to American missionary agencies that had "shewn themselves the enemies of the Established Church."[14] The Federalist arguments for the separation of church and state could not be tolerated in a Canada desirous of maintaining the connection to God's chosen empire of Great Britain. Like Stuart before him, Strachan noted that discipline was required if Canadian society hoped to emulate Britain's God-honoring legacy.[15] Whatever rhetoric the anti-Reserves camps used, Strachan argued Christianity was "a continual lesson of obedience to the laws and submission to constituted authorities"—not a characteristic he believed American-based faith possessed. Their Revolution had proven them "enemies to regular Government," seek-

---

13. Stuart, "Letter," 118.
14. Strachan, *Speech*, 28. Strachan granted one of the more evangelical denominations tacit support: "Of the Wesleyan Methodists I have spoken with approbation, as well as of their Teachers and Preachers, because they appear, in as far as I have seen, exceedingly respectable, and the friends of piety and good order; but I cannot approve of those Methodists who get their Teachers and Preachers from the United States." Strachan, *Speech*, 27.
15. "Even in those remote parts of the country, where the Methodist Itinerants are the most active, so soon as the population is sufficiently compact to admit and require the ministrations of a regular Clergyman, he finds his congregation increasing by the gradual accession of their more respectable adherents" Excerpt from Jacob Mountain's Memorial to King George IV as found in Ryerson, *The Clergy Reserve Question*, 12.

ing rather to "destroy the influence of religious principles, and to pull down religious establishments"[16]

In his 1825 eulogy for the Anglican Bishop of Quebec, Jacob Mountain, Strachan sounded a clarion call: "if the Imperial Government does not immediately step forward with efficient help, the mass of the population will be nurtured and instructed in hostility to our Parent Church, nor will it be long till they imbibe opinions anything but favourable to the political Institutions of England."[17] Thus, one of the preeminent issues behind the Clergy Reserves was fear that a weakened Anglican Church could not protect colonists from being seduced by individualistic Christianity. A version of the faith too attached to the trends of the age and foreign politics, rather than the ancient faith spread by a godly Empire. A citizenry lacking proper religious instruction could not make educated choices in matters of faith. Society would decline, and before long, even the ardently faithful would be beyond hope because all their choices would be conducive to, and influenced by, the environments in which they were raised.

Therefore, we return to Bethune's warning that unless "restitution is made, or penitence at least is expressed by a God-fearing people," the future of the colony was bleak. Without the discipline and oversight of a well-funded British and Protestant church,

---

16. Strachan, *Speech*, 28.
17. "Even when churches are erected, the Minister's influence is frequently broken or injured by numbers of uneducated itinerant Preachers, who leaving their steady employment, betake themselves to preach the Gospel from idleness, or a zeal without knowledge, by which they are induced without any preparation, to teach what they do not know, and which, from their pride, they disdain to learn. When it is considered that the religious teachers of the other denominations of Christians, a very few respectable Ministers of the Church of Scotland excepted, come almost universally from the Republican States of America, where they gather their knowledge and form their sentiments, it is quite evident, that if the Imperial Government does not immediately step forward with efficient help, the mass of the population will be nurtured and instructed in hostility to our Parent Church, nor will it be long till they imbibe opinions anything but favourable to the political Institutions of England. It is only through the Church and its Institutions, that a truly English character and feeling can be given to or preserved in any Foreign possession" Strachan's Eulogy of Bishop Mountain as found in Ryerson, *The Clergy Reserve Question*, 14.

"public disquiet will be the heritage of coming generations." Even if funds were used to support non-sectarian education throughout the colony (the stated desire of most anti-Reserves groups), such education "without the life and light of religion" would create only further enmity.[18] The legacy of non-religious (read non-Anglican) education would be "a bitter testimony to the dangers of a little learning," and the colonial world of British North America "shall have scepticism and infidelity rampant in the land."[19] For those invested in Anglican supremacy, the issue was aligning colonial faith with the proven godly character of the British constitution so that other dangerous ideas did not overwhelm the soul of society.

Secularizing the Reserves & Religious Freedom

The irony is that the concerns of those opposed to the Reserves were quite similar. For them, the inclusion of denominations like the Congregationalists, Baptists, Methodists, Free Presbyterians, and United Presbyterians safeguarded genuine faith against narrow party interests. Bethune, Strachan, Chalmers, and Stuart were concerned that the lack of Reserves meant that the individual would be raised in a land of weak faith. Thus, whatever choice each colonist made in regard to his or her religion would be the result of negligent Christian education. Those in the anti-Reserves camps argued it was the Clergy Reserves that were really to blame. This misguided policy actually weakened colonial faith by monopolizing one version of Christianity over other legitimate expressions, thereby disadvantaging numerous other loyal Christian

---

18. "Caleb Hopkins . . . spoke in favour of outright repeal of the Clergy Reserves and their devotion to education." Moir, *Church and the State*, 53.

19. Bethune, *Clergy Reserves*, 13. Strachan (*Speech*, 41) agrees: "Do we ever find any upright trustworthy, or giving Religion a thought, unless they have been educated in it from their childhood? . . . But it is unnecessary to argue upon this subject, or to say more than to recall to Christians the positive commands of Scripture—to teach Children the fear of God—to bring them up in the fear and admonition of the Lord: While therefore King's College will be open to all denominations of Christians, it will nevertheless possess a religious character."

voices dedicated to supporting Imperial interests.[20] These Christians saw the Reserves as an outdated and ill-fitting Imperial policy at best, and tyrannical abuse of clerical power at worst. Their arguments proposed that greater inclusion of differing religious views posed no threat to Imperial interests and strengthened the burgeoning nation's desire for progress. However, they agreed with their opponents' concerns about individualism harming true faith. Whereas Bethune, Chalmers, and Strachan worried over the common person's attention to matters of faith, those in favour of disbanding the Reserves worried about one specific man's attention to faith.

The strength of the pro-Reserves party was that Clergy Reserves were instituted by the late King George III (d. 1820). Thus, to call them into question was akin to challenging the ruling of the respected monarch. However, Reformers argued the actual origin of the ruling came from an 1819 charter, posthumously applied to George III and obtained under dubious circumstances by Lord

---

20. "And we humbly beg leave further to represent to your majesty, that, apart from the objections entertained by the great majority of your majesty subjects in Canada, to religious endowments, by which certain favoured denominations of Christians, are kept in connection with the state, and thereby placed in a position of superiority over others, the present disposition of the revenue derived from the clergy reserves investments is manifestly unjust. That the entire revenue derived from the investments made before the passing of the imperial act three and four, Victoria, chapter 78, has been there by assigned to the churches of England and Scotland, to the exclusion of the Wesleyan Episcopal and New Connexion Methodist, the free Presbyterian Church of Canada, the United, Presbyterian Church, the Baptist, Congregationalists, and other religious bodies, whose pastors have an equal claim to the designation of a protestant clergy, with those of the clergy of the churches of England and Scotland." Earl of Elgin & Kincardine, *Despatch*, 4. On the loyalty of the Episcopal Methodists specifically: "They are not Republicans; neither are they infected with republican principles; nor have they come 'almost universally from the Republican States of America.' *Seven eighths* of the religious teachers among the dissenters, are British born subjects. And out of the whole body of the Methodist itinerant preachers, who seem to be the principal butt of the Doctor's hatred, there are only eight who have not been *born and educated* in the British dominions. And of those eight *all* except *two* have become naturalized British subjects according to the statute of the Province." Ryerson, *The Clergy Reserve Question*, 18. Italics part of the original quote.

Bathurst. In his appeal to Imperial officials, Egerton Ryerson noted the Anglicans "acquired the superintendence and control of the Clergy Reserves, not by the Statute 31st George the Third, [as believed by most] but by a Charter obtained Under the auspices and by the recommendation of Lord Bathurst—notorious as well as odious for his high church exclusion and bigotry."[21]

This has two very important elements to consider. First, the exclusive rights of the Anglican (and later Presbyterian) Church to the funds were not a wish of the late King but were the political machinations of a man whose desires for Anglican supremacy were well documented. Second, the character of the charter, written as it was in London, did not correspond to the reality of colonial life. Rather, the charter was shown to shape colonial life in confining ways that desired to consciously advantage one church over the others; with no attention paid to the wants or religious desires of the people. Those opposing the Reserves argued they "did not originate with any disappointed party either in Canada or elsewhere," crying out for a sturdier Anglican presence. In fact, the desire for Reserves did not originate in Canada at all! Nor did it "originate with even a liberal whig" but originated "with no less personages than that high Churchman, Earl Bathurst himself."[22]

The Clergy Reserves were thus argued to be an external policy enacted by a powerful person from outside of Canada clearly doing so to advantage his own religious beliefs. Therefore, if the argument for institutions was that they safeguarded citizens from their baser inclinations, the Reformers were able to show that the institutions of colonial religion were really the result of one man's "bigoted" desires. That, in the words of Ryerson and others, was religious tyranny.[23] It forced a singular ideology upon masses who possessed little financial or practical recourse to oppose the

---

21. Ryerson, *The Clergy Reserve Question*, 5.
22. Ryerson, *The Clergy Reserve Question*, 7.
23. "That this violent infraction of the rights of your petitioners, and of the Canadian people generally, was accompanied by circumstances of the deepest treachery, so derogatory to the character of a civilized government, and so calculated to alienate the minds of the people and annihilate all confidence in their rulers, that the parties implicated therein deserve yet to be impeached." Various Authors, "Petition to the Provincial Parliament," 1.

choice. It was less tyrannical and more civilized, fraught with perils as this may be, for individual freedom of conscience to reign rather than living in a world where one man's desires could hold so much sway.

Conclusion

The issues discussed in this reflection are far removed from the issues of our present age. However, in this story, we can draw parallels between the nineteenth-century Clergy Reserve issues and the twenty-first-century church adherence issues. For those invested in the religious institutions of our age, the abandoning of institutional faith is characterized as "secularization." This story teaches there are always those on the outside of even the most celebrated religious structures who have been neglected and oppressed by those very same institutions. For those who have experienced disenfranchisement, the ability to secularize religious institutions feels like freedom and empowerment.

When the Clergy Reserves were eventually secularized, faith in Canada did not disappear. Neither did morality, social cohesion, or material blessings. If anything, genuine religion deepened as Imperial authorities recognized the landscape of Canadian religion was a decision best made by Canadians, not for Canadians. Today, as back then, it is incumbent upon Christians to understand the ways institutional structures fail to protect or benefit all Canadian lives. After all, in the second half of the nineteenth century, the waning of institutional structures like the Reserves meant the waxing of others dedicated to genuine faith, education, and beneficial social reforms. Their successes were based less on the institutional demands of a few and more on the religious freedom of the many. Despite Bethune's condemnations, Canadians of the nineteenth century were not "robbing from God." They were simply removing an institution deemed unfit and problematic. Perhaps the non-religious of today are, likewise, not abandoning God but finding their spiritual happiness in a shifting landscape that no longer requires the old structures.

Bibliography

Bethune, A. N. *The Clergy Reserve Question As Now Agitated: In A Letter to the Hon. Robert Baldwin, M.P.* Toronto, F. Plees, 1850.

Cornelissen, Louis. "Religiosity in Canada and its Evolution from 1985 to 2019." *Statistics Canada*, 28 October 2021. N.p. Online: https://www150.statcan.gc.ca/n1/pub/75-006-x/2021001/article/00010-eng.htm.

Earl of Elgin and Kincardine. *Despatch to Earl of Grey Forwarding an Address of the Legislative Assembly of Canada to Her Majesty on the subject of the Clergy Reserves.* London: Harrison and Son, 1851.

Moir, John S. *Church and the State in Canada West, 1841–1867.* Toronto: University of Toronto Press, 1959.

Pennings, Ray, and Jenisa Los. "The Shifting Landscape of Faith in Canada." *Cardis*, 23 November 2022. N.p. Online: https://www.cardus.ca/research/faith-communities/reports/the-shifting-landscape-of-faith-in-canada.

Snyder, Timothy. *On Tyranny: Twenty Lessons from the Twentieth Century.* New York: Tim Duggan, 2017.

Strachan, John. *A Speech of the Venerable John Strachan D.D. Archdeacon of York in the Legislative Council Thursday Sixth of March 1828 on the Subject of the Clergy Reserves.* York: Robert Stanton, 1828.

Stuart, John. "Letter to the SPG, 26 September 1786." In *Kingston before the War of 1812: A Collection of Documents*, edited by Richard A. Preston, 118. Toronto: Champlain Society, 1959.

Ryerson, Egerton. *The Clergy Reserve Question: As a Matter of History—A Question of Law—and a Subject of Legislation; In a Series of Letters to the Hon. W.H. Draper.* Toronto: J. H. Lawrence, 1839.

Thompson, Nicole. "More Canadians than ever have no religious affiliation, census shows." *The Canadian Press*, 27 October 2022. N.p. Online: https://www.cbc.ca/news/canada/kitchener-waterloo/canadian-census-religious-affiliation-none-1.6631293.

Various Authors, "Petition to the Provincial Parliament to Abolish the Rectories and to Appropriate the Proceeds of the Clergy Reserves to the Support of Common Schools." Unknown: Unknown, n.d.

Embracing the Possibilities of Resurrection

Jay Mowchenko
Briercrest University, Caronport, SK, Canada

It is no surprise and the truth is clear: the decline in Canadian Christian belief and practice is long-term, systemic, and does not seem to be stopping. Whether it is because the Canadian Church as a whole has not yet found the right solution, or God for some reason has decided not to act is unclear. How deep the valley will be is anybody's guess.

Over the past decades, there have been many different creative attempts to reverse the decline. They seem to fit within the categories that Jim Collins uses to describe an organization in freefall:

1. Endlessly pursuing silver bullets—"game changers" that promise to quickly catalyse breakthrough;
2. Grasping for leaders to be saviours;
3. Hasty, reactive behaviour and emotion-driven decision-making;
4. Cries for "revolution" [or in the church context, "revival"];
5. Hype preceding results – overpromising and underdelivering as opposed to the opposite;
6. Initial excitement leading to inevitable disappointment;
7. Confusion and cynicism;
8. Constant restructuring[1]

I am confident that each reader will be able to supply examples of many of these from their own lived experience. It is important for those concerned by this trend to recognize that the decline is not purely a local or personal thing. Whatever is causing this, the scope of it is certainly more expansive than any organizational leader or theological tradition. So, for those carrying the responsi-

---

1. Collins, *How the Mighty Fall*.

bility for turning their particular church around, or for those blaming their pastor or denominational leader for the struggles of their local church, this larger perspective can perhaps soften their critique. This is a long-term, multi-denominational, national trend.

Further to that, what if, in the divine economy, this decline is not meant to be reversed? What if God has a purpose for what is occurring? What if these attempts at reversing the decline are signs that we have succumbed to the temptations Marva Dawn warns against?

> Both the concern for "church growth" and the concern for survival (which sometimes are the same thing) lead to many of the tactics of the fallen powers, such as competition, the overwhelming pressures on church leaders to be successful, reduction of the gospel for the sake of marketing and so forth.[2]

As we continue to ride the slide downward, how could a Christological perspective inform this journey? What if the decline of the Christian institutional church in Canada is serving to bring the people of God closer to the posture and mind of Jesus? Perhaps the work of breaking down the former established order is necessary to clear the ground for new adaptations to flourish? Mac Loftin, in his September 2023 article in *The Christian Century*, contends that this is the case:

> Who Jesus is is the one who effaces himself so that others can take his place, the one who allows himself to be transformed into what he is not . . . This means that we're called to look for Jesus not by turning inward to the already known but by leaving the familiar behind and seeking him in an unknown future . . . If the church is the body of Christ, and if Christ is the one who effaces himself to make room for others, then the anxious desire to preserve Christianity . . . at all costs is revealed as an enormous theological error . . . Christianity—at least Christianity as we in the West have known it—may very well be in its last days. But Christians should reject the temptation to rage against the dying of the light, whether by weaponizing state power against

---

2. Dawn, *Powers, Weakness, and the Tabernacling of God*.

those bringing change or by cozying up to the rich and powerful and well-connected. Permanence was never our calling.[3]

So what? What does it mean? What are we to do?

Perhaps the first step is to embrace the journey of grief, a la Elizabeth Kubler-Ross,[4] encouraging those still within Canadian institutional Christianity to face what aspects of grief or lament they must address to move towards acceptance and be released to engage in new possibilities. Whether that is denial and isolationism, anger and bargaining or despair, unresolved grief may be much of what is driving our current religious polarization. Loftin legitimizes the need to process grief and loss in his article, along with an invitation to move forward:

> The loss of the traditional and familiar is certainly a cause for mourning, as the death of anything cries out to be mourned. But—having consecrated these passable forms with our gratitude—we must allow our mourning to pull us forward, elsewhere, on toward the unknown. We as Christians are called to have faith that while our wanderings will bring risk and danger, we might also find grace in being altered by what comes, in listening with attention to the incomprehensible words of the strangest stranger as perhaps the word we have been listening for.[5]

I would invite those who occupy leadership positions within the existing Church hierarchies to embrace this as their calling for the next several generations—to provide palliative care and support to the people and organizations that need to continue to decline while also holding space for what comes next. Forty percent of Canadians still hold to Christian belief, even though far fewer engage in regular religious practice.[6] So this work will still be important and challenging as people continue to struggle through the process of caring for what remains, grieving and letting go.

While the Christian narrative embraces the idea of surrendering to death and giving up one's life for another, this also eventually

---

3. Loftin, "A Better Response," n.p., emphasis added.
4. Kubler-Ross, *On Death and Dying*.
5. Loftin, "A Better Response," n.p.
6. See this sobering article from 2016: Hiemstra and Stiller, "Religious Affiliation," n.p.

leads to resurrection. Elaine Heath and Charles Kiser describe the transition we seem to be experiencing in this more hopeful way:

> We are at the forefront of a new reformation, one that is freeing the Christian faith from the sinful structures of patriarchy, racism, classism, many phobias, and exploitive forms of mission and evangelism. The new reformation is about the emergence of a generous, hospitable, equitable form of Christianity that heals the wounds of the world.[7]

Seen in this light, decline and possibly death can have a cleansing, freeing function, releasing the followers of Christ from the bondage of institutional power and privilege. If this is the case, what might that new reformation look like? How might the explorer of new territory move forward in search of a resurrection for Canadian Christianity? I have been intrigued by the path that Randy Woodley offers in his "Missiological Imperatives":

1. There is no place we can go where Jesus is not already present and active.
2. Since Jesus is active everywhere, the first responsibility of mission among any culture is not to teach, speak or exert privilege but to discover what Jesus is already doing in that culture.
3. Realize that God expects two conversions out of every missional encounter: 1) our conversion to the truths in their culture, and 2) their conversion to the truth we bring to the encounter.
4. Our humility as servant of Jesus should naturally lead to us first convert to the truths in their culture wherever we see Jesus is at work.
5. Through the work of culture guides (people of that culture), earnest study, prayer and experiential failures, it is our responsibility to first adapt to and then embrace their culture, and as much as possible, their worldview,
6. Realize that conversion is both instantaneous and a process (the biblical data of salvation is becoming wholly healed) and think through these implications as you begin to consider your timelines. Then, throw out your timelines.

---

7. Kiser and Heath, *Trauma-Informed Evangelism*, 61.

7. During this time, also read, study, and discuss with others the ways that you can continue to deconstruct your own worldview and culture. This is a long, painful, and yet freeing process.
8. Our own process of conversion may take years, so be patient with yourself and with God. When and if they invite us to share the gospel they have noticed us living out, then the process formally known as cultural contextualization should occur.
9. Their process of conversion may take years, so be patient.[8]

First, I take heart from Woodley's assertion that even as the institution declines, *Jesus is not absent!*

Second, I encourage us to take seriously the invitation to consider that God is at work in the growth of the "nones" in Canada. There must be something redemptive and compelling about the pursuits and lifestyle that draws Canadian people to think and live the way they do. An attentive missionary might be able to observe and tease out the difference between Christological principles and practices and those that conflict with the Jesus Way.

The challenge that is most poignant comes in Woodley's third point—that conversion must go both ways. Perhaps the "nones" are on to something—something that the current vision and practice of Canadian Christianity is missing? We might begin by sifting through the critiques that are currently being offered of the Church, and see if there are grains of truth that invite a response. It is this point that seems most lacking in historic and current postures within the institutional Church. There is a common attitude that the Truth (note the capital "T") resides within the Church and that outsiders have nothing to offer, which leads to a defensive posture by default. Instead of seeing themselves as bringing the light of the gospel to a lost and dying world, perhaps Canadian Christians could begin with a diligent search for what is good and right in their communities, find people of peace,[9] and partner with them in working for the common good.

---

8. Woodley, *Indigenous Theology and the Western* Worldview, 108–109.
9. A la Luke 10:5–6.

Fourth, Woodley's challenge to patience is extremely appropriate. Rooted in the Indigenous peoples' patient yet persistent pursuit of treaty solutions, this word "patience" should have a meteoric impact on our pursuit of quick fixes. The journey of decline and resurrection for the Canadian Church is multi-generational and will likely require many more generations before it comes to fruition. Lord willing, it will include a deep and meaningful transformation of the relationship between the Church and First Peoples.

Finally, I take hope in the idea that this decline might just be successful in accomplishing the cleansing and restoring work that Heath and Kiser describe. Who knows? The conversion process might result in our *own* conversion, restoring Christian communities in Canada back to the original fervour and radical compassion that was evident in the early Church. Canadian Christians might one day be able to return to that place, where people from outside would ask of them, "Why do you live and love the way you do?"[10]

Bibliography

Collins, Jim. *How The Mighty Fall: And Why Some Companies Never Give In*. Illustrated edition. New York, NY: HarperCollins, 2009.

Dawn, Marva J. *Powers, Weakness, and the Tabernacling of God*. 1st edition. Grand Rapids, MI: Eerdmans. 2001.

Hiemstra, Rick, and Karen Stiller. "Religious Affiliation and Attendance in Canada." *In Trust Magazine*, January 2016, n.p. Online: https://www.intrust.org/in-trust-magazine/issues/new-year-2016/religious-affiliation-and-attendance-in-canada.

Kiser, Charles, and Elaine Heath. *Trauma-Informed Evangelism: Cultivating Communities of Wounded Healers*. Grand Rapids: Eerdmans, 2023.

10. Kreider, *The Patient Ferment of the Early Church.*

Kreider, Alan. *The Patient Ferment of the Early Church: The Improbable Rise of Christianity in the Roman Empire*. Grand Rapids: Baker Academic, 2016.

Kubler-Ross, Elisabeth. *On Death and Dying*. 13th edition. New York, NY: Macmillan Publishing Company, 1970.

Loftin, Mac. "A Better Response to the Decline of the Christian West." *The Christian Century*, 13 September 2023, n.p. Online: https://www.christiancentury.org/article/features/better-response-decline-christian-west?utm_source=newsletter&utm_medium=email&utm_content=A%20better%20response%20to%20the%20decline%20of%20the%20Christian%20West&utm_campaign=ni_newsletter.

Woodley, Randy. *Indigenous Theology and the Western Worldview: A Decolonized Approach to Christian Doctrine*. Acadia Studies in Bible and Theology. Grand Rapids: Baker Academic, 2022.

PROSPECTS FOR CHRISTIANITY AFTER CHRISTIAN HEGEMONY

Mark A. Noll
University of Notre Dame, Indiana, USA

Post-Christendom Studies is an appropriate journal for essays discussing recent surveys that measure religion in contemporary Canada. Whether Statistics Canada reporting a sharp decline in Christian identification from 2001 (77 percent) to 2021 (53 percent) and a corresponding rise in "no religion" identification (16 percent in 2001; 35 percent in 2021)—or Cardus-Angus Reid identifying only 35 percent of Canadians as either religiously committed (16 percent) or privately religious (19 percent)—Canada presents a natural case for considering the prospects for Christianity in a post-Christendom society.[1]

As a historian working primarily on US subjects, but with also a long-standing interest in Canada, I was accustomed to stress historical differences between Canada, with its Protestant and Catholic varieties of "Quasi Christendom," and the US, with what might be called a history of "White Protestant Privilege" exercised through voluntary means and a formal separation of church and state.[2] Now, however, especially with a number of social and cultural developments in the two countries converging, I am inclined to see more similarity between the two societies. In particular, both Canada and the US seem to be experiencing a rapid dis-

---

1. "The Canadian Census: A Rich Portrait of the Country's Religious and Ethnocultural Diversity," *The Daily*, 26 October 2022, 11–16. Component of Statistics Canada catalogue no. 11-001-X; and Angus Reid-Cardus, "Canada across the religious spectrum" n.p.

2. Noll, *What Happened to Christian Canada?*

mantling of their slightly different forms of "Christian hegemony."[3]

The situations, of course, are still not exactly the same. Canada's Medical Assistance in Dying (MAID) has established a national legal provision that is unlikely to become law throughout the *entire* United States. Although religious identification and religious practices differ considerably by region in both countries, no American state has formalized the militant *laïcité* that now prevails in Quebec. Most obviously, all-out media focus on "evangelical" (really, white evangelical Protestant) support for Donald Trump's radical populism makes this one American religious-political connection much more salient than any of the real, but less obsessively tracked, religious-political connections in Canada.[4] To be sure, if that US connection would contribute to an actual tide of violence or play a role in sustaining an all-out insurrection, then religious divergence between the two countries would once again loom large.

Despite these and other continuing differences, convergences are strikingly apparent. Although the US has not officially adopted an ideology of multiculturalism, the DEI (diversity, equity, inclusion) emphasis, with its own ideal of multiculturalism, has gained unofficial standing in many places. In both countries a common degree of public acceptance of gay marriage is another sign of life after Christendom. Concerning abortion and despite rulings of the US Supreme Court and legislation in several Republican-led states, Americans, in general, seem almost as willing as Canadians to break from the traditional Christian prohibition.

Social scientists have provided specific evidence of convergence by describing a United States rapidly catching up with Canada in religious self-identification. Although American Chris-

---

3. For a lucid statement describing the "dismantling of the Christian hegemony in Canada," see Stackhouse, "Anglophone Canada," 40–51 (quotation, 48).

4. As a check on media enthusiasm, however, a recent survey indicates that US white evangelical congregations are *less* politically engaged than white mainline Protestant, Black Protestant, or Roman Catholic congregations: Public Religion Research Institute, "Religion and Congregations in a Time of Social and Political Upheaval" n.p.

tian identification remains higher and the "none" identification lower, the trend in the Canadian direction is unmistakable. A recent Pew Research Center study records a decline in Christian identity from 90 percent in 1972 to 63 percent in 2022 and a rise in those without a religious affiliation from 5 percent to 29 percent over the same period.[5]

Without the same degree of social scientific precision, the conclusion is nonetheless inescapable that in both societies other concerns (wealth, leisure, entertainment, self-actualization, sport, group identity, group resentments) now exert far more influence than traditional features of Christian societies: concern for virtue (public and private), emphasis on moral guilt and spiritual redemption, prominent attention to theological matters like sin and grace, the practices of prayer and Bible reading, regular church attendance.

Churches and other Christian institutions in both countries have also become targets for their part in subjugating racial minorities. Especially since the report from Canada's Truth and Reconciliation Commission, reproach directed at majority Protestants and Catholics for dehumanizing First Nations families in residential schools has become almost as pervasive as the American indictment of white Christians for sanctioning the enslavement of Black people and then supporting systematic discrimination after slavery.

In short, although historical developments are not identical, in both nations, the instinctive deference to Christianity that prevailed as late as the post-War period is no more. Even when Christianity now features prominently, as with attention to white American evangelicals, the evolution of "evangelical" from primarily a religious category to primarily a social-cultural interest indicates the passing of *Christian* hegemony.

In order to imagine a positive place for Christianity in societies where historical forms of Christian influence are gone—or if lingering, strongly contested—it is possible to consider whether

---

5. Pew Research Center, "Modeling the Future of Religion in America," n.p.

selected features of Christian hegemony can be recast in post-Christian terms, but also whether historical Christian expressions that did not share in cultural hegemony point a way to prospects for the future.

In the first instance, noteworthy Canadian efforts, as by the non-partisan think tank Cardus, have labored to define "school choice" as a just provision for all religious, ideological, or interest-group communities, and not just for schools organized by Christian denominations.[6] Similar efforts have not been as clearly argued in the US, but they are increasingly present in a range of efforts from Christian authors contending for general "freedom of religion" instead of freedom intending to preserve inherited Christian privilege.[7]

Hidden in survey data charting the rapid decline of Christian identification are also clues for a different way forward for Christianity beyond Christian hegemony. A recent report from Statistics Canada has shown that the rate of Christian self-identity among First Nations Canadians lags only slightly behind the general public (43 percent vs. 53 percent), that for Métis the number (51 percent) is about the same, and that for Inuit it is considerably higher (71 percent).[8] Similar studies from the Pew Research Center register higher figures for Christian identification among Black and Hispanic Americans than for the population at large.[9]

Examples for what North American Christianity, shorn of Christendom or Christian privilege, might look like now abound. Terry LeBlanc of the North American Institute for Indigenous Theological Studies has explained how First Nation Christians have been extracting themselves "from the confines of Western church traditions and structures, including modes of governance and worship." In his account, these efforts are expressing a particularly Native Christianity that is not beholden to earlier assump-

---

6. As an example, See Van Pelt, "Charting New Horizons for Independent Education in Canada," n.p.
7. For example, Witte, et al., *Religion and the American Constitutional Experiment*.
8. Statistics Canada, "Religion by Indigenous Identity," n.p.
9. Pew Research Center, "Faith American Black Americans," n.p. Pew Research Center, "The Shifting Religious Identity of Demographic Groups," n.p.

tions about "civilization and Christianity." Instead they embrace "the triple restorative mandates of right relationship with God and other spiritual powers, right relationship with one another in the human community and right relationship with and relatedness to the rest of creation, of which humanity is but a part."[10]

South of the 54th parallel, Roberto Chao Romero has witnessed a similar move among Hispanic believers who are defining their faith without worrying about Protestant privilege. As he views this process, it is a rebuke to both the Christian right—"white Christian nationalism . . . that conflates the church with US civil religion and rejects immigrant Christians as undesirable newcomers and even illegitimate believers"—and also the progressive Christian left that limits "faith to social activism, while de-emphasizing personal transformation and deep spiritual encounter with the Holy Spirit." His vision for the Christian future does not require "a complete eradication of Euro-American church traditions," but rather a "sifting [of] racial sin" that leads to "rebuilding the North American church based upon the diverse cultural treasures of the various ethnic groups which will comprise the US church in the coming decades."[11]

In such accounts, prospects for Christianity in the US and Canada do not feature nostalgia, resentment, anger, or fear. Instead, they hold out the possibility that authentic faith need not depend on the structures of the past, whether Canada's Quasi-Christendom or the US's White Protestant Privilege. Among other benefits, realizing such a possibility would facilitate opportunities for mutual learning from the many Christian communities around the world that have never enjoyed Europe's structural Christendom or its North American adaptations. It would also relativize what for believers sounds like the bad news from social scientists and encourage recognition of Christian resources that were neglected when believers were in charge.

---

10. All references in this paragraph are from LeBlanc, "First Nations Canada," 38.
11. All references in this paragraph are from Romero, "The Future of Christianity in North America," 427, 435.

Bibliography

Angus Reid-Cardus. "Canada across the religious spectrum." 18 April 2022, n.p. Online: https://angusreid.org/canada-religion-interfaith-holy-week.

LeBlanc, Terry. "First Nations Canada." In *Christianity in North America*, edited by Kenneth R. Ross, et al., 25–39. Edinburgh: Edinburgh University Press, 2023.

Noll, Mark A. *What Happened to Christian Canada?* Vancouver: Regent College Publishing, 2007.

Pew Research Center. "Faith American Black Americans." 16 February 2021, n.p. Online: https://www.pewresearch.org/religion/2021/02/16/faith-among-black-americans.

———. "Modeling the Future of Religion in America." 13 September 2022, n.p. Online: https://www.pewresearch.org/religion/2022/09/13/modeling-the-future-of-religion-in-america.

———. "The Shifting Religious Identity of Demographic Groups." 12 May 2015, n.p. Online: https://www.pewresearch.org/religion/2015/05/12/chapter-4-the-shifting-religious-identity-of-demographic-groups.

Public Religion Research Institute. "Religion and Congregations in a Time of Social and Political Upheaval." 16 May 2023, n.p. Online: https://www.prri.org/research/religion-and-congregations-in-a-time-of-social-and-political-upheaval.

Romero, Robert Chao. "The Future of Christianity in North America." In *Christianity in North America*, edited by Kenneth R. Ross, et al., 427–40. Edinburgh: Edinburgh University Press, 2023.

Stackhouse, Jr., John G. "Anglophone Canada." In *Christianity in North America*, edited by Kenneth R. Ross, et al., 40–51. Edinburgh: Edinburgh University Press, 2023.

Statistics Canada. "Religion by Indigenous Identity." 26 October 2022, n.p. Online: https://www150.statcan.gc.ca/t1/tbl1/en/tv.action?pid=9810028801.

The Daily. "The Canadian Census: A Rich Portrait of the Country's Religious and Ethnocultural Diversity." 26 October 2022, 11–16. Component of Statistics Canada catalogue no. 11-001-X.

Van Pelt, Deani. "Charting New Horizons for Independent Education in Canada." *Cardus*, 13 December 2023, n.p. Online: https://www.cardus.ca/research/education/perspectives-paper/charting-new-horizons-for-independent-education-in-canada.

Witte, John, et al. *Religion and the American Constitutional Experiment*. 5th ed. New York: Oxford University Press, 2022.

Learning from a More Secular Future: Insights from Aotearoa New Zealand

Lynne Taylor
University of Otago, Dunedin, New Zealand

Writing from the Future

I am writing to you from the future—literally. Whatever time it is in Canada, you can be sure that we are at least 18 hours ahead of you: Aotearoa New Zealand's East Cape is the first place to welcome each day and each new year.

I am also writing from a different kind of future. According to the latest Census data, over half of Canadians are still affiliated with Christianity. Down here, that seems like a lot. In Aotearoa New Zealand, we dipped below 50 percent Christian in 2006, and by 2018, the number of people of no religion was higher than the number of Christians. (We are still waiting on the 2023 data to be released.)

In this brief essay, I begin by discussing some characteristics of religion, church attendance, spirituality, and secularization in Aotearoa New Zealand, before offering two contrasting ways that we could consider the situation we now find ourselves in. I then turn to the Canadian context, noting points of similarity and difference. I conclude by offering hopeful signs from research that demonstrates a continued (perhaps increasing) interest in spirituality and that people do still embrace the Christian faith. This research from a more "secularized" context can provide insights for Canadian churches and Christians as they navigate changed and changing times.

The New Zealand Context

Declining Religious Affiliation

In New Zealand, affiliation with Christianity was fairly stable from the earliest census in 1848 (when the total population was less than 100,000) until the late 1960s. A steady decline followed: from 89 percent Christian in 1966 to 38 percent Christian in 2018 (Figure 1).

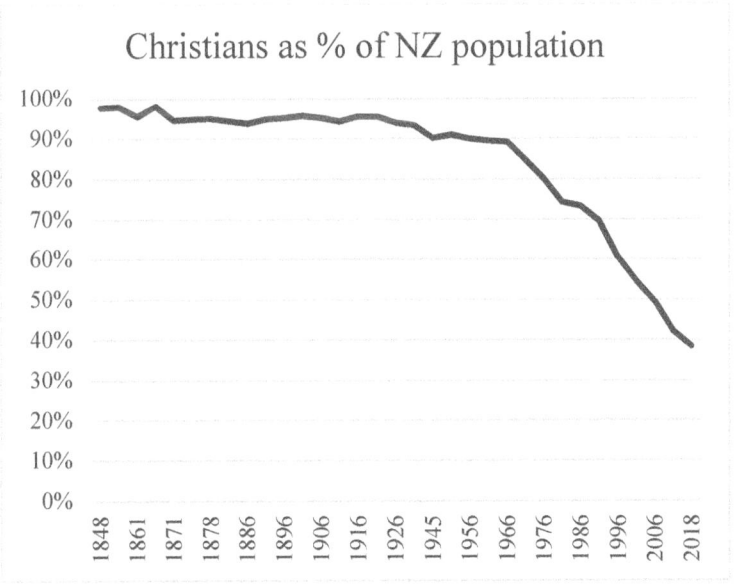

Figure 1: Christian religious affiliation in New Zealand[1]

The decline in Christianity was very partially offset by an increase in proportions of people of other faiths (rising to 7.5 percent in 2018). But it was the proportion of people of "no religion" that was growing markedly. In fact, between 2013 and 2018, the number of religiously unaffiliated people overtook the number of Christians, reaching 48 percent to Christianity's 38 percent in 2018. (See Figure 2.)

1. Data from New Zealand Census. Spreadsheet maintained by author.

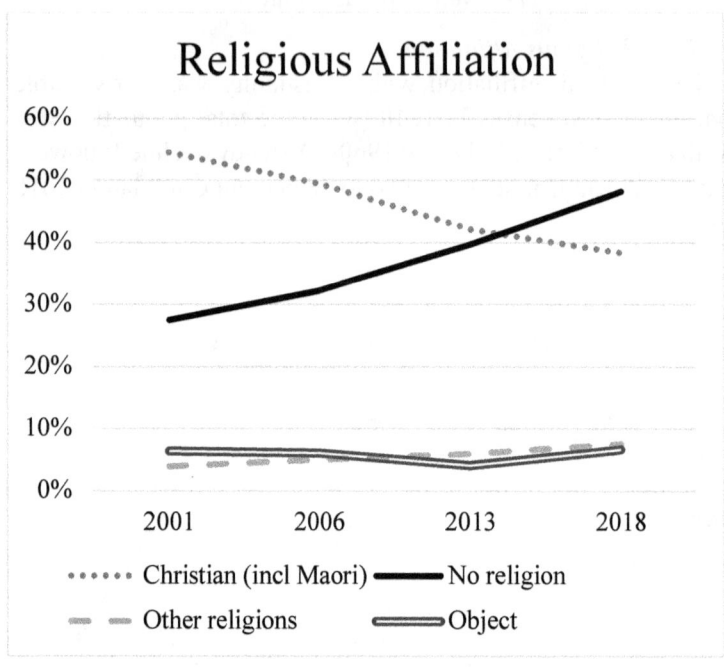

Figure 2: Religious affiliation, New Zealand 2001–2018[2]

Declining Church Attendance
Of course, religious affiliation is just one measure of secularization. Another relatively easy measure is church attendance. This, too, is declining in most denominational contexts in New Zealand. I am most familiar with the Baptist data, where the denomination (mostly) grew until the early 2000s. However, much of this growth was as a direct result of former attenders of mainline churches transferring to Baptist churches. Further, that growth was increasingly unable to keep pace with population increase. Later, much of the growth came in ethnic churches (and then in multicultural churches) where immigrants, particularly from the

---

2. Data from New Zealand Census. Spreadsheet maintained by author.

less secularized Pacific, masked what would otherwise have been a decline in attendance in both percentage and real terms.

From 2003, the picture has been one of general decline. Even excluding the COVID-19 period, there was a nearly 25 percent drop in attendance of Baptist churches between the peak in 2004 and 2019. (See Figure 3.)

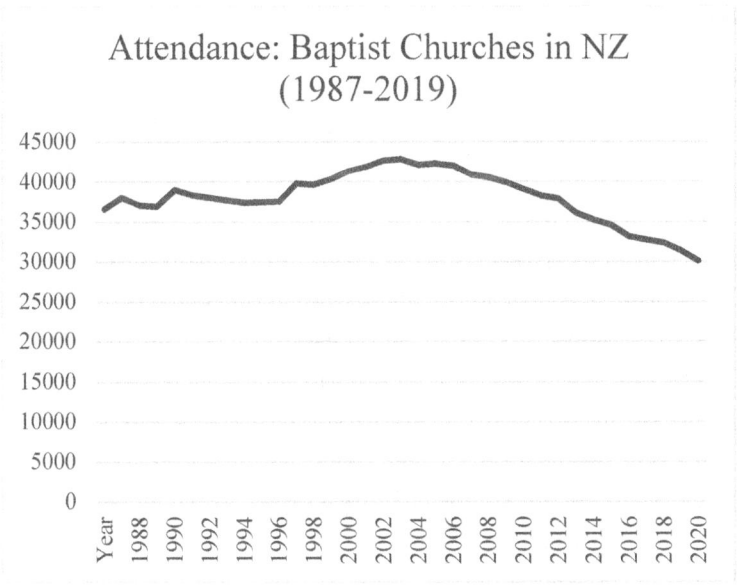

Figure 3: Baptist church attendance 1987–2019[3]

Post-COVID Decline
In the post-COVID period, declines in church attendance have been dramatic. Anecdotally, I frequently hear the figure of a one-quarter drop in church attendance from pre-COVID to today. The 2022 Baptist statistics certainly showed such a decline, although there seems to have been some recovery in 2023.[4]

---

3. Data from Baptist churches annual statistical returns. Spreadsheet maintained by author.
4. The 2023 data is yet to be fully captured and reported.

Across many areas of life, COVID-19 acted as an accelerant: acting for good and for ill; sparking the best and the worst of actions and attitudes, and everything in between. The pandemic also sped up processes that were already inevitable. This happened in relation to church attendance in New Zealand, where even following the easing and removal of gathering restrictions, many found that their priorities had changed along with their habits. Fewer people attend church, and those who do attend are likely to do so less frequently.

Declining Influence of Christianity on Society
Unsurprisingly, Christianity does not hold an overt place of influence in Aotearoa New Zealand. While, in many ways, influence is deeply embedded in society and laws, there are no opportunities or expectations that a "Christian perspective" will be sought or valued in the marketplace. Churches and Christians experience this in different ways, as mainline churches lament a loss of influence or invitation to speak into public discourse, and more evangelical churches struggle with social values that seem at odds with the moral stances that they hold to.

Problem or Condition?
This new reality can be viewed in at least two ways. Christianity's minority status and declining influence can be seen either as a problem or as a condition.[5]

Viewing it as a problem implies that it is something that needs to be solved, something that can be solved. The church in New Zealand has been seeing declining religious affiliation and declining church attendance as a problem for several decades—a problem that they have been unsuccessful in "solving" despite rigorous and sustained efforts. The same is true of declining social and political influence; this can also be seen as a problem that needs to be solved, perhaps by seeking to "take control of the levers of government."[6]

---

5. Here I am drawing on Brian Harris' helpful distinction between "problems" and "conditions." See Harris, "Towards a 21st Century Church," n.p.
6. Fitch, "Why Christian Nationalism is Anathema," n.p.

A more helpful way of viewing this new reality is not as a problem but as a condition: a changed circumstance that is a new reality. It is important to note that in Aotearoa New Zealand, there is more to this condition as well: a deep appreciation of what indigenous Māori call wairuatanga (spirituality).

Spirituality is Valued

In 1840, a treaty was signed in New Zealand between the indigenous Māori and newly arrived European settlers. While Māori have certainly suffered the ill effects of colonization, among the impacts of the Treaty/Te Tiriti, particularly recently, has been a burgeoning valuing of spirituality, recognized as foundational to our nation. This has resulted in both an increased general attention to spirituality, as well as legislated and cultural appreciation of te ao Māori (the Māori world) and wairuatanga.

As Troughton and Fountain note, "an indigenous Māori cultural renaissance and state attempts to recognise the moral imperative of decolonisation . . . have resulted in new languages of spirituality shaping both law and politics."[7] To illustrate, recent government legislation has acknowledged the spiritual connection that Māori have with the land. Spirituality is widely viewed as a crucial dimension of health and wellbeing.[8] Karakia (ritual prayer) is frequently included in state occasions, schools, and business and community meetings.[9]

While certainly not embraced by all, such attention to wairuatanga has permeated society and contributed to a greater appreciation of spirituality. This is part of what Charles Taylor would call the "changed conditions of belief" in New Zealand.[10]

In addition, migration has brought with it people of faith. As Filipino Catholics and Middle Eastern Muslims immigrate,

---

7. Troughton and Fountain, "An Insecure Secularity?" 529. In late 2023, a new coalition government was elected that seems intent upon rolling back many recent attempts at honoring the Treaty. See, for instance, Duff, "'A Massive Unravelling,'" n.p.
8. Durie, "A Maori Perspective on Health," 6.
9. Troughton and Fountain provide a concise description of how these are outworked. Troughton and Fountain, "An Insecure Secularity?" 532–34.
10. Taylor, *A Secular Age*, 3.

Aotearoa's landscape changes. For instance, in Auckland, New Zealand's largest city, 74 percent of Roman Catholics were born overseas.[11] Migrants are also younger and welcoming new generations of children. This further complexifies the landscape as some Christian denominations and other religions grow while most denominations decline.

A Secular Context

All this points to New Zealand as being deeply secularized. Drawing on Charles Taylor's framing, we are experiencing declining religious affiliation and attendance; declining influence of Christianity in the public square; and changed conditions of belief.[12] The latter includes a deeper appreciation of spirituality. But that is New Zealand. How about Canada?

On Canada

Canada is clearly experiencing a decline in religious affiliation, although it still remains considerably more religiously affiliated than New Zealand. As Stuart Macdonald and Brian Clarke noted in 2017, "decline in Christian affiliation, membership, and participation started [in Canada] in the 1960s and has picked up pace rapidly since then."[13] Canada's current rate of decline continues to be high; in fact it is increasing.[14]

In Canada, rates of affiliation are also unevenly distributed across the country, with "Canadian nones . . . more likely to reside

---

11. McDonald et al., *Insights from the 2023 Church Life Survey New Zealand*, 8.
12. Taylor, *A Secular Age*, 3.
13. Macdonald and Clarke, *Leaving Christianity*, 11.
14. At -2.31 percent, the relative percentage change per year is comparable with the decline experienced in New Zealand between 2006 and 2013 (-2.26 percent pa). In Canada, this is up from -1.35 percent pa between 2001 and 2011. By contrast, between 2013 and 2018, NZ's rate of decline had decreased to -1.87 percent pa. Unlike NZ, therefore, Canada's rate of decline is still increasing. (Here, I am using the calculation employed by Andrew Reyngoud, "An analysis of the variations and future implication," 58. This takes into account the two-year delay in New Zealand's 2013 Census, a result of the February 2011 Christchurch earthquake.)

in . . . British Columbia" than elsewhere in Canada.[15] While New Zealand shows marked denominational variation across different regions, based largely on historical migration/settlement patterns, there is not such a regional variation in overall affiliation. In Canada, this difference means that insights drawn from one region may not translate directly to another; but like NZ, BC may also act as a sort of "future" for the rest of Canada.[16]

How to Respond?

Declining Christian religious affiliation, church attendance, and influence can all contribute to a lack of confidence among churches and Christians. Analyzing longitudinal research on churches in Australia, Ruth Powell notes that what she calls "collective confidence creates a positive spiral," contributing to an environment that welcomes newcomers.[17] The inverse is also true. This final section outlines some lessons from a "future" that, while highly secularized, can nonetheless be a site of spiritual vitality. The essay then concludes with suggestions for how one might live in these changed and changing times. I hope that these insights about a future where people remain open to exploring Christian faith can work to build a collective confidence in Canadian churches, towards a hopeful future, albeit one that is necessarily different than the present and the past.

A recent study of "Faith and Belief" among a representative sample of people in Aotearoa New Zealand showed that most people can imagine themselves further investigating faith and/or spirituality. Specifically, 75 percent of respondents pointed to "experiencing a personal trauma or significant life change"; 68 percent to "exploring different spiritual practices"; and 66 percent to "seeing first hand people who live out a genuine faith or spirituality" as

---

15. Dilmaghani, "Canadian Religious Trends," 626.
16. However, historian Lynne Marks asserts that BC was never actually particularly religious, as white settlers "found a unique freedom to be actively irreligious." Marks, *Infidels and the Damn Churches*, 4. Also, see Byassee and Lockhart, *Better Than Brunch*, 2–3.
17. Powell, *What Makes a Healthy Church?* See also Powell et al., *Models of Church Vitality*.

things that might attract them to explore faith or spirituality for themselves.[18] My own PhD research on why previously unchurched Australians become Christians today confirms that exploring different spiritual practices and seeing people live out authentic faith are significant among the things that attract people to Christianity. Engaging in spiritual practices works to form faith.[19] A desire for what I call relational authenticity, and a witnessing of it in the lives of Christian friends acts as both a key motivation for and an enhancer of faith exploration.[20]

The Faith and Belief study also tells us that it is really only 18 percent of the population who are cold towards Christianity, either having "strong reservations about Christianity and . . . no interest in it" (12 percent) or being "passionately opposed" to it (6 percent).[21] Worth noting here are the generational differences: it is the younger generations who are "slightly more likely than their older counterparts to be warm towards Christianity (30% Gen Z, 28% Gen Y cf. 24% Gen X, 25% Baby Boomers)."[22] Growing up in more secular times does not result in a lack of openness to, or negative perceptions of, Christianity. It seems more a case of indifference than antagonism. While this is heartening, we should also recognize that there may well be painful stories behind the greater resistance in older generations. Also noteworthy is that intolerance, judgementalism, behavior and morals, hypocrisy and unwelcome evangelism were all named as "aspects of Christianity and/or Christians that [at least 5 percent of all] respondents find problematic or challenging."[23] How Christians act and respond and what they say are important.

18. McCrindle, *Faith and Belief Te Patapātai Whakapono*, 19.
19. Taylor, "Our Doing Becomes Us," 332–41.
20. Taylor, "A Multidimensional Approach," 33–51.
21. McCrindle, *Faith and belief Te Patapātai Whakapono (Short Report)*, 31.
22. McCrindle, *Faith and belief Te Patapātai Whakapono (Long Report)*, 41.
23. McCrindle, *Faith and belief Te Patapātai Whakapono (Long Report)*, 45. These responses were coded from qualitative data. Further analysis would be worthwhile.

The study also points to yearnings and needs that churches are (or at least should be) well-placed to meet.[24] A desire for a deeper sense of community and belonging, a longing to feel hopeful about the future, and a sense of hopelessness about the state of the planet. These are all things that churches ought to be able to resource and strengthen. Doing so requires a church that is not preoccupied with its own structures and members but is actively listening to those beyond their walls, seeking to understand the yearnings and to resource the spirituality and well-being of those around them.

As always the church is invited to act with faithfulness, humility, faith, hope and love. And the greatest of these is love. Our secularized context is not a problem that can be solved. Rather, it is a condition that we now live in.

As a result of this new reality, there are several questions that churches and Christians can be asking. The question is not "how do we solve this problem?" "But how do we live now?" "How might we be the church today?" "How do we faithfully witness to God's goodness and grace?" "How do we sustain the spirituality, and faith development of people in our churches?" And "How might we resource those beyond our churches who want to embrace or resource their spirituality? Of those who want to live flourishing lives?"

Bibliography

Byassee, Jason, and Ross A. Lockhart. *Better Than Brunch: Missional Churches in Cascadia.* Eugene, OR: Wipf and Stock, 2020.

Dilmaghani, Maryam. "Canadian Religious Trends: Secularization, Polarization, or Free-Rider Exclusion?" *Social Compass* 65. 5 (2018) 626–49.

---

24. See McCann and Bechsgaard, *The Sacred in Exile.*

Duff, Michelle. "'A Massive Unravelling': Fears for Māori Rights as New Zealand Government Reviews Treaty." *The Guardian*, 1 December 2023, n.p., online: https://www.theguardian.com/world/2023/dec/02/fears-for-maori-rights-as-new-zealand-government-reviews-waitangi-treaty.

Durie, M. H. "A Maori Perspective on Health." *Social Science and Medicine* 20.5 (1985) 483–86.

Fitch, David. "Why Christian Nationalism is Anathema to the Mission of God," *Fitch's Provocations*, 21 November 2023, n.p. online: https://davidfitch.substack.com/p/why-christian-nationalism-is-anathema.

Harris, Brian. "Towards a 21st Century Church: Four Assumptions to Challenge." 23 April 2019, n.p. online: https://brianharrisauthor.com/towards-a-21st-century-church-four-assumptions-to-challenge.

Macdonald, Stuart, and Brian Clarke. *Leaving Christianity: Changing Allegiances in Canada Since 1945.* Advancing Studies in Religion 2. Montreal: McGill-Queen's University Press, 2017.

Marks, Lynne. *Infidels and the Damn Churches: Irreligion and Religion in Settler British Columbia.* Vancouver: University of British Columbia Press, 2017.

McCann, Gillian, and Gitte Bechsgaard. *The Sacred in Exile: What It Really Means to Lose Our Religion.* New York: Springer, 2017.

McCrindle. *Faith and Belief Te Patapātai Whakapono: Exploring the Spiritual Landscape in Aotearoa New Zealand (Long Report).* Wilberforce Foundation (2023).

———. *Faith and Belief Te Patapātai Whakapono: Exploring the Spiritual Landscape in Aotearoa New Zealand (Short Report)*. Wilberforce Foundation (2023).

McDonald, Barry, et al. *Insights from the 2023 Church Life Survey New Zealand: The Perspective, Character and Values of Church Attendees across Aotearoa New Zealand*. Church Life Survey NZ (Auckland: 2023).

Powell, Ruth. *What Makes a Healthy Church?* NCLS Research (Sydney: 2021).

Powell, Ruth, et al. *Models of Church Vitality: A Literature Review (Occasional Paper)*. NCLS Research (Sydney: 2019).

Reyngoud, Andrew. "An Analysis of the Variations and Future Implication of Changes in Demographics That Have Been Experienced by NZ Baptist Churches between 1989 and 2019." Masters of Applied Theology Thesis, Carey Baptist College, 2023.

Taylor, Charles. *A Secular Age*. Cambridge: Harvard University Press, 2007.

Taylor, Lynne. "A Multidimensional Approach to Understanding Religious Conversion." *Pastoral Psychology* 70.1 (2021) 33–51.

———. "Our Doing Becomes Us: Performativity, Spiritual Practices and Becoming Christian." *Practical Theology* 12.3 (2019) 332–41.

Troughton, Geoffrey, and Philip Fountain. "An Insecure Secularity? Religion, Decolonisation and Diversification in Aotearoa New Zealand." *The Round Table* 112.5 (2023) 529–42.

Home Away from Home:
An Outsiders' Reflection on the 2021 Canadian Census

David Tarus
Association for Christian Theological Education in Africa, Nairobi, Kenya

Joshua Robert Barron
Association for Christian Theological Education in Africa, Nairobi, Kenya

The last century has seen seismic shifts in global Christianity. Africa, Asia, Latin America, and Oceania are Christianity's current home. Lamin Sanneh, Andrew F. Walls, Philip Jenkins, Patrick Johnstone, Joel A. Carpenter, Kwame Bediako, Jehu J. Hanciles, and many others have written extensively on this phenomenal shift of the Christian faith.

In the last century, there has been notable population growth in these regions accompanied by rapid accession to Christian faith, resulting in an increase in the Christian population. Jenkins provides an example from Kenya:

> [I]n the lands that would become Kenya, the population in 1900 was a mere one million, but that figure has now [in 2014] swollen to around 40 million, in little over a century. By 2050, Kenya could have 80 million people or more. In 1900, there were three Europeans for every African; by 2050, there should be three Africans for every European. In consequence, the absolute number of African believers soared, from just 10 million in 1900 to 500 million by 2015 or so, and (if projections are correct) to an astonishing billion by 2050. Put another way, the number of African Christians in 2050 will be almost twice as large as the total figure for all Christians alive anywhere in the globe back in 1900.[1]

---

1. Jenkins, "Changes and Trends," 17, 18.

The growth of Christianity in the Global South is not tied to a close connection between Christianity and secular powers. That form of Christianity, usually referred to as *Christendom*, is a cultural and "territorial expression of Christianity"[2] or "the territorial Empire of Christ,"[3] in which Christian identity—though not necessarily Christian faith—is adopted, or rather assumed, "essentially in terms of law and custom."[4] This *"corpus Christianum"* was conceived as "a single society in which the whole of public and private life was to be controlled by the Christian revelation"[5]—and with its laws and customs supported by the secular state. But when the secular state provides backing to Christianity, it does so in the presence of skeptical observers and outspoken critics who view such support with suspicion because of their apprehensions regarding the convergence of secular authority and religious objecttives. Frequently, Christianity flourished in regions where it constituted a minority religion, thriving amidst challenges, such as opposition, poverty, and frequent persecution. Interestingly, and contrary to general expectations, "it was precisely as Western colonialism ended that Christianity began a period of explosive growth that still continues unchecked."[6]

The kind of Christianity that took root bears a different flavor from the one bequeathed to local communities by Western missionaries. Gone are the days when it can be assumed that "the American" (or Canadian or British or other European) "way of life [is the] supreme expression of Christianity."[7] In Africa, the Christian faith is authentic, charismatic, practical, and real. It is a faith that offers tangible solutions to real-time challenges facing people. Andrew Walls memorably noted that "the urge to make Chris-

---

2. Walls, "The Eighteenth-Century Protestant Missionary Awakening," 41.
3. Walls, "The Translation Principle in Christian History," 37.
4. Walls, *The Missionary Movement from the West*, 8. Sierra Leonean theologian Jehu Hanciles similarly defines Christendom as "the experience and understanding of Christianity as a territorial and tribal faith." Hanciles, *Beyond Christendom*, 3.
5. Newbigin, *Foolishness to the Greeks*, 101.
6. Jenkins, *The Next Christendom*, 70.
7. Hastings, "The Clash of Nationalism and Universalism," 32.

tianity a place to feel at home, rooted in a people's culture, life and language, is of the heart of the gospel because it is a fundamental of the gospel that God takes us as we are, simply on grounds of what Christ has done."[8] Christianity has experienced phenomenal growth in the Global South precisely where and when the local people have found, or made, Christianity to be *a place to feel at home*. This contrasts with the current reality in Canada, where there is a real "decline in the practice of religious activities, both collectively and individually, and in the importance of religious and spiritual convictions in how people live their lives"[9] and "surveys consistently report that people believe that religion does more harm than good."[10] Prior to the mid-1940s, acceptance "of the basic tenets of Christianity was assumed to be part of the worldview of any educated Canadian" whereas today there is "a kind of chasm . . . between religion and society" in Canada.[11] But in contemporary Africa, faith still profoundly influences the way individuals lead their lives, with religion and daily existence intricately connected and inseparable. As John Mbiti observes, Africans carry their religion to the fields, to educational institutions, to the marketplace, and even to the parliament; the African person is "notoriously religious."[12]

The profile of global Christianity has evolved, with a Christian individual more likely to be a Black woman in Eldoret, Kenya, or a Hispanic woman in São Paulo, Brazil, rather than a White man or woman in Toronto, Canada. This demographic portrait of Christianity is anticipated to remain unchanged in the near future. As the Canadian Survey shows, there is still a massive growth of "racialized groups in Canada," representing 16.1 percent of Canada's population.[13] Jenkins avers that by 2050 "even our

---

8. Walls, "Africa and Christian Identity," 11; Walls is alluding to the titular theme of Welbourn and Ogot, *A Place to Feel at Home*.
9. Statistics Canada, *The Canadian Census*, 13.
10. Zurlo, *Global Christianity*, 79.
11. Bramadat, "Beyond Christian Canada," 3–4.
12. Mbiti, *African Religions and Philosophy*, 1.
13. "The Canadian Census: A Rich Portrait of the Country's Religious and Ethnocultural Diversity," *The Daily*, 26 October 2022, 2. Component of Statistics Canada catalogue no. 11-001-X.

'Euro-American' Christians will include Congolese believers living in Paris, Chinese in Vancouver, Korean in Los Angeles, and Nigerians almost anywhere."[14] Given that "immigrants make up the largest share of the population in over 150 years and continue to shape who we are as Canadians,"[15] it is crucial to investigate the impact of immigration on the decline or growth of Christianity in Canada.

In Canada, as in Europe, the United States, and Australia, Christianity has experienced a swift decrease, as the Census indicates. The figures reveal a diminishing trend, with 77.1 percent of the population identifying with the Christian religion in 2001, 67.3 percent in 2011, and further dropping to 53.3 percent in 2021. Interestingly, around 12.6 million people, constituting one-third of the population, reported having no religious affiliation,[16] an increase from 19 percent in 2004.[17] The Census also pointed out the possible decrease in religious beliefs among individuals who move to Canada and among children born in Canada.[18] Other demographers found that Canada "was 98% Christian in 1990 and 63% in 2020," with a drop to 53 percent expected all too soon.[19] It is crucial to investigate the underlying reasons for this phenomenon. That said, immigration offers hope for the Christian faith in Canada and beyond.

In an article titled "New Canadians Promise Renewal for Christian Churches," published in the *Edmonton Journal* on 7 April 2012, the author stated that "immigrants from the Southern Hemisphere are already altering Canada's religious landscape, by-

---

14. Jenkins, "Changes and Trends," 18.
15. "The Canadian Census: A Rich Portrait of the Country's Religious and Ethnocultural Diversity," *The Daily*, 26 October 2022, 14. Component of Statistics Canada catalogue no. 11-001-X.
16. "The Canadian Census: A Rich Portrait of the Country's Religious and Ethnocultural Diversity," *The Daily*, 26 October 2022, 2, 12, 13. Component of Statistics Canada catalogue no. 11-001-X.
17. Reimer, "A Demographic Look at Evangelical Congregations," 1.
18. "The Canadian Census: A Rich Portrait of the Country's Religious and Ethnocultural Diversity," *The Daily*, 26 October 2022, 13. Component of Statistics Canada catalogue no. 11-001-X.
19. Zurlo, *Global Christianity*, 78.

passing the shrinking mainline Protestant churches while infusing Catholic and Pentecostal congregations with devout newcomers."[20] The Census agrees on this trend:

> Catholics are the largest Christian denomination in Canada, with 10.9 million people (29.9%) in 2021. The United Church (3.3%) and the Anglican Church (3.1%), two other Christian denominations, each had more than 1 million people in Canada. Orthodox Christians (1.7%), Baptists (1.2%), and Pentecostals and other Charismatics (1.1%) were the other Christian denominations most often reported.[21]

From the Census, it is clear that global migration is a contemporary expression of missions. Despite certain indications of the adverse effects of migration on Christianity (e.g., "Immigration is one of the key drivers of non-Christian religions"[22]), "migrants have literally been prime movers of Christian expansion; every Christian migrant is a potential missionary!"[23]

The January/February 2024 issue of *Faith Today*, Canada's premier evangelical magazine, featured a discussion on modern missions. In one of the articles, the writer quotes Joel Gordon, who serves with the Evangelical Fellowship of Canada (EFC), reflecting on some lessons learned from a trip to Türkiye for the World Evangelical Alliance's *Future of the Gospel* forum: "We have many Christians coming from Nigeria where there's 10,000 to 50,000 people in a church . . . they are coming with ideas, and gifts, and energy, and vibrancy, and music and other ways of living out the gospel that need to be embedded in the Canadian context in order for us to be more effective in reaching all people."[24] As a result of this disconnect, "African churches in diaspora largely remain the locus of identity, community and security pri-

---

20. Wittmeier, "New Canadians Promise Renewal."
21. "The Canadian Census: A Rich Portrait of the Country's Religious and Ethnocultural Diversity," *The Daily*, 26 October 2022, 12. Component of Statistics Canada catalogue no. 11-001-X.
22. "The Canadian Census: A Rich Portrait of the Country's Religious and Ethnocultural Diversity," *The Daily*, 26 October 2022, 14. Component of Statistics Canada catalogue no. 11-001-X.
23. Hanciles, *Migration*, 1; emphasis original. He later repeats "all migrants are potential missionaries," 29.
24. Fitz-Gerald, "Rethinking Global Mission," 31.

marily for African immigrants."[25] David Guretzki, also from EFC, contends that Canadian Christians have not fully connected with certain ethnic groups present in Canada because they are isolated or separated from them. Hence, they miss the contributions of such to the growth of the Church in Canada: "The Nigerians, Ghanaians and Chinese, for example, may have a whole lot more to say about evangelizing Canada."[26]

In *Word Made Global: Stories of African Christianity in New York City*, Mark Gornik notes that when he began writing his book, he could not locate "a single article or book on the subject of African churches in North America."[27] This assertion speaks to the scholarly neglect of the contributions of immigration to North American Christianity. There is a lack of efforts to engage with immigrants and understand their perspectives in order to enhance Christianity in North America. Lee Beach asks some critical questions connected to this concern: "Will the emergence of a robust church in South America, China, and Africa have an impact on the church in Canada?" "Can missionaries from South America, China, or Africa help the church in Canada to reach Canadians?"[28] The answer is yes.

The presence of multitudes of "African immigrant Christians . . . in the West is [definitely] proving to be of great missionary significance."[29] If existing local Canadian church congregations are to directly benefit from this, rather than only new congregations serving only immigrants, Rich Janzen et al. contend that Canadian congregations must develop a vision to be intentional about "immigrant integration," emphasizing that "immigrants and Canadian born" Christians are necessarily "mutual resources for each other."[30] But is the Canadian church (and the Western church generally) a welcoming church? Is it open to really listen and learn from the rest? How should the church in the West reorient itself

25. Adogame, *The African Christian Diaspora*, 80
26. Fitz-Gerald, "Rethinking Global Mission," 31.
27. Gornik, *Word Made Global*, 15.
28. Beach, "New Models of Ministry," 49.
29. Kwiyani, *Sent Forth*, 16.
30. Janzen, et al., "Integrating Immigrants into the Life of Canadian Urban Christian Congregations," 444.

to benefit from the church in the Global South? Is the non-Christian West really ready for the Christian rest? How might Western Christians benefit from the Christian immigrants who have moved there? And how should the church in the Global South position itself to be of more significant influence globally?

I (David) was also present at the WEA *Future of the Gospel* forum mentioned above. I observed that despite the presence of a few Africans, such as myself, there was no tangible intention to include African voices in the discussions. At one time, one of the participants insisted that Africans should not just be at the table where discussions happen; they must be in the kitchen where the "meal" is prepared. Otherwise, they are on the menu. It seems little has changed since 1976, when John Mbiti chastised Western theologians for ignoring African voices. He wrote,

> We have eaten theology with you; we have drunk theology with you; we have dreamed theology with you. But it has been all one-sided; it has all been, in a sense, your theology . . . We know you theologically. The question is, "Do you know us theologically?" . . . You have become a major subconscious part of our theologizing, and we are privileged to be so involved in you through the fellowship we share in Christ. When will you make us part of your subconscious process of theologizing?[31]

The words of John Mbiti find greater meaning in today's multiethnic Canada. The rest of the world has come to Canada. The "cultural diversity" which had been "built into the church early in the apostolic period" has now returned to the universal Church and today "Africa and Asia and Latin America are part of North America, and they will never go away."[32] The unreached people groups are no longer in the remote jungles of Africa but within the bustling cities of Canada. Canadian churches, individual Christians, Christian organizations, and others need to make space for the other, to carefully listen and learn, and to re-envision the church, theological education, and life to serve the millions of Canadians who have found a home far away from home. And perhaps just as African Christian Theology has arisen from the effort

---

31. Mbiti, "Theological Impotence," 16–17.
32. Walls, *The Missionary Movement from the West*, 224, 246.

to "interpret Christ to the African in such a way that he feels at home in his faith,"[33] the churches of Canada can develop a Canadian Christian Theology that can allow today's post-Christendom Canadians to also feel at home in Christian faith.

Bibliography

Adogame, Afe. *The African Christian Diaspora: New Currents and Emerging Trends in World Christianity*. London: Bloomsbury Academic, 2013.

Beach, Lee. "New Models of Ministry in Canada as a Response to the Decline of Western Christianity." In *The Globalization of Christianity: Implications for Christian Ministry and Theology*, edited by Gordon L. Heath and Steven M. Studebaker, 31–51. McMaster Theological Studies Series 6. Eugene, OR: Pickwick, 2014.

Bramadat, Paul. "Beyond Christian Canada: Religion and Ethnicity in a Multicultural Society." In *Religion and Ethnicity*, edited by Paul Bramadat and David Seljak, 1–29. Toronto: University of Toronto Press, 2009.

Fitz-Gerald, Julie. "Rethinking Global Mission." *Faith Today*, 1 January 2024, n.p. Online: https://www.faithtoday.ca/Magazines/2024-Jan-Feb/Rethinking-global-mission.

Gornik, Mark R. *Word Made Global: Stories of African Christianity in New City*. Grand Rapids: Eerdmans, 2011.

Hanciles, Jehu J. *Beyond Christendom: Globalization, African Migration and the Transformation of the West*. Maryknoll, NY: Orbis, 2008.

———. *Migration and the Making of Global Christianity*. Grand Rapids: Eerdmans, 2021.

---

33. Sawyerr, "What Is African Theology?," 26.

Hastings, Adrian. "The Clash of Nationalism and Universalism within Twentieth-Century Missionary Christianity." In *Missions, Nationalism, and the End of Empire*, edited by Brian Stanley, 15–33. Studies in the History of Christian Missions. Grand Rapids: Eerdmans, 2003.

Janzen, Rich, et al. "Integrating Immigrants into the Life of Canadian Urban Christian Congregations: Findings from a National Survey." *Review of Religious Research* 53 (2012) 441–70.

Jenkins, Philip. "Changes and Trends in Global Christianity." In *The Globalization of Christianity: Implications for Christian Ministry and Theology*, edited by Gordon L. Heath and Steven M. Studebaker, 15–30. McMaster Theological Studies Series 6. Eugene, OR: Pickwick, 2014.

———. *The Next Christendom: The Coming of Global Christianity*. Oxford: Oxford University Press, 2002.

Kwiyani, Harvey C. *Sent Forth: African Missionary Work in the West*. American Society of Missiology Series 51. Maryknoll, NY: Orbis, 2014.

Mbiti, John S. *African Religions and Philosophy*. 2nd ed. London: Heinemann, 1990.

———. "Theological Impotence and the Universality of the Church." In *Third World Theologies*, edited by Gerald H. Anderson and Thomas F. Stransky. Mission Trends 3. New York: Paulist, 1976.

Newbigin, Lesslie. *Foolishness to the Greeks: The Gospel and Western Culture*. London: SPCK, 1986.

Reimer, Sam. "A Demographic Look at Evangelical Congregations." *Church and Faith Trends* 3.2 (2010) 1–21.

Sawyerr, Harry. "What is African Theology?" In *A Reader in African Christian Theology*, edited by John Parratt, 29–36. London: SPCK, 1997.

The Daily. "The Canadian Census: A Rich Portrait of the Country's Religious and Ethnocultural Diversity." 26 October 2022, 11–16. Component of Statistics Canada catalogue no. 11-001-X.

Walls, Andrew F. "Africa and Christian Identity." *Mission Focus* 6 (1978) 11–13.

———. "The Eighteenth-Century Protestant Missionary Awakening in Its European Context." In *Christian Missions and the Enlightenment*, edited by Brian Stanley, 22–44. Studies in the History of Christian Missions. Grand Rapids: Eerdmans, 2001.

———. *The Missionary Movement from the West: A Biography from Birth to Old Age*. Edited with a Preface by Brian Stanley. Foreword by Gillan Mary Bediako. Studies in the History of Christian Missions. Grand Rapids, Michigan: Eerdmans, 2023.

———. "The Translation Principle in Christian History." In *Bible Translation and the Spread of the Church*, edited Philip C. Stine, 24–39. Leiden: Brill, 1990.

Welbourn, Frederick Burkewood and Bethwell A. Ogot. *A Place to Feel at Home: A Study of Two Independent Churches in Western Kenya*. Oxford: Oxford University Press, 1966.

Wittmeier, Brent. "New Canadians Promise Renewal for Christian Churches." *Edmonton Journal*, 6 April 2012, n.p. Online: https://edmontonjournal.com/news/new-canadians-promise-renewal-for-christian-churches.

Zurlo, Gina A. *Global Christianity: A Guide to the World's Largest Religion from Afghanistan to Zimbabwe*. Grand Rapids: Zondervan Academic, 2022.

Religion and the Canadian Census Data: Some Reflections from Across the Pond

Mark J. Cartledge
London School of Theology, London, UK

Introduction

I write as a Caucasian male British Anglican, a clergyperson in the Church of England, a practical theologian, and a scholar of global Pentecostalism. I lead an interdenominational evangelical school, which has also been impacted by the changing landscape of Christianity in the UK. We have a mixed and diverse group of students from around the world, accessing education both online and on campus.[1]

In this paper, I offer some brief reflections from my own context. I intend to describe the basic picture that is present in the Canadian data and identify some possible explanations before suggesting some possible ways of responding to the picture that are constructive for the church. My conclusion summarizes key points and suggests how the conversation might be developed.

The Canadian Census Data

The basic picture presented when the 2011 and 2021 data are compared is a sobering one, to say the least. It is clear that Christian affiliation is still in the majority (19.3 million in 2021), which represents just over 53.3 percent of the population. However, this is a decrease in claimed Christian affiliation when placed alongside previous surveys, compared to 67.3 percent in 2011 and 77.1 per-

---

1. See https://lst.ac.uk.

cent in 2001.[2] Roman Catholic Christians dominate (29.9 percent in 2021), while other denominations or traditions are 3 percent or less. Whereas in other contexts, Pentecostals and Charismatics might be outgrowing Roman Catholics, in Canada they are still relatively small at 1.1 percent. What is of interest is that 7.6 percent of the population (or 2.8 million) reported Christian affiliation without any specific denomination, thus suggesting that these people are unaffiliated with regard to specific Christian communities or traditions. In addition, 12.6 million Canadians, or one-third of the population, report no religious affiliation, which is a rise from 16.5 percent in 2001 to 23.9 percent in 2011 and to 34.6 percent in 2021. Immigrants contribute to this number (21.5 percent from 2011 to 2021), but it is boosted significantly by people who have lost their religious affiliation in recent years. Clearly, other religious traditions are growing (e.g., Islam at 1.8 million, 4.9 percent of the population), which is a significant growth from 2011 (2.0 percent of the population), but it is still relatively small as a religious group within the overall landscape. By contrast, indigenous spirituality is relatively tiny (81,000 or 0.2 percent of the population), with the majority being First Nations people.

What is also of note is that in the vast landmass of Canada, these religious affiliations vary considerably. Roman Catholicism is the most widely distributed Christian tradition across all provinces and territories (with the exception of Nunavut). Quebec is just about majority Roman Catholic at 53.8 percent, but this has fallen considerably from 74.7 percent in 2011. The United Church does better in Atlantic provinces, and the Anglicans have a stronger presence in Nunavut, Newfoundland and Labrador. Yukon (59.7 percent) and British Columbia (52.1 percent) are the least religiously affiliated, thus suggesting greater secularization tendencies in these geographical areas. Non-Christians are present in greater numbers in eastern cities and metropolitan areas, for example, Ontario (16.3 percent) and British Columbia (13.7 percent), suggesting that secularization provides a greater degree of

---

2. The UK Census data of 2021 shows that 46 percent, or 27.5 million of the population describes themselves as Christian. For all data references see https://www.ons.gov.uk/datasets/TS030/editions/2021/versions/1.

religious plurality. The urban landscape attracts a greater density of immigrants so it is unsurprising that greater levels of non-Christian religions are also present in the urban setting.

Explanations

The data is always useful as a snapshot of what is happening at a given time in a specific context. It answers some very basic "what" type questions. Of course, what it cannot do is answer the "why" type questions. This is where scholars attempt to place data into an ongoing academic conversation in order to understand the explanations of what is happening. Sociologists of religion often discuss various explanations for the reduction in religious affiliation in Western democracies. The most prominent theory is often referred to as secularization and has a number of proponents and different emphases.[3] Essentially, the stronger version of the theory that predicted the virtual eradication of religion has not been fulfilled and shows no sign of being fulfilled in the near future. However, the versions of the theory that stress a gradual reduction in formal religious participation over time do appear to have an empirical basis. Over time, each generation is less religiously affiliated than the previous generation. As formal participation in a religion declines so religious illiteracy increases. There is an increasing ignorance of what religion actually looks like from the inside, so to speak.

Those who do profess a religious affiliation are increasingly diverse, and this is especially seen in the growth of non-Christian religions in the global north, especially Islam. Numbers of adherents are still small in terms of the overall population, but over time these numbers will grow, especially if immigration policies continue to allow the flow of migrants from the global south. What is fascinating to observe is that the Pentecostal and Charismatic church migration does not appear to have had a significant impact

---

3. See the discussions by Casanova, *Public Religions in the Modern World*; Davie, *Religion in Britain Since 1945*; Davie, *The Sociology of Religion*; Martin, *On Secularization*; Brown, *The Death of Christian Britain*; Bruce, *God is Dead*; and Bruce, *British Gods*.

on the religious landscape of Canada, unlike its impact in the global cities in Europe where the growth in Christian affiliation is largely due to African diaspora churches.[4]

There is no real surprise in the growth of the "nones" in a secularized Western context. In Canada, approximately 12.6 million people or a third of the population self-designate as being of no religion, which is a rise from 16.5 percent in 2001 and 23.9 percent in 2011.[5] With increased religious illiteracy comes increased disinterest. What is intriguing is the lack of affiliation with specific denominational traditions for those who do have some Christian sense of identity (affinity with Christianity but not the church). The group that still wishes to be called Christian but on their own terms. This is perhaps what some sociologists have termed "individualization," namely the idea that the individual stands at the centre of the religiously constructed reality and does not defer to authority outside of the self.[6] When this is linked to a consumerist approach to religion, it leads to what Matthew Guest has called "neoliberal religion."[7] People in this category float between religious worlds and choose what is convenient and palatable according to their own shifting and developing tastes. What I think is perhaps disconcerting is the fact that this attitude is also present among those who also affiliate with specific Christian traditions, suggesting that socialization is an increasingly important concept for understanding the transmission of Christian beliefs and values.

Responses

It is inevitable that the churches are keen to understand this picture and to formulate their responses because of the importance of their mission in the world. If numbers are reducing at speed, what can be done, or what should be done and why? In any context, num-

---

4. See Cartledge, et al., *Megachurches and Social Engagement*, 77–80.
5. The UK data shows an increase of 12.0 percent from 25.2 percent or 14.1 million in 2011 to 37.2 percent or 22.2 million in 2021.
6. See Ziebertz, ed., *Religious Individualization and Christian Religious Semantics*.
7. Guest, *Neoliberal Religion*.

bers matter since large numbers are associated with success, influence, and future survival. A number of reflections are offered to the churches in the Canadian context from this side of the transatlantic "pond."

The British context is probably ahead of Canada by a few years. We are bolstered by an established church, the Church of England, which has certain privileges, but which is also in serious decline, especially outside of cities and among non-Evangelical churches. The churches that are growing tend to be among conservative or charismatic Evangelicals or specialist traditional churches like cathedrals. Other churches, like the Methodist, United Reformed Church, Church of Scotland, and Baptist, are suffering a serious decline in numbers attending worship services. Independent, migrant Pentecostal churches are growing in urban centres but via immigration, not through reverse mission. Reverse mission is claimed by these groups, but there is very little evidence of indigenous, Caucasian British people joining these churches, except perhaps through marriage and in very small numbers. The tension with wider society is especially prominent around LGBTQIA+ matters, and it is expected that the cultural split will be accentuated within Evangelicalism, especially over the next decade, thus potentially leading to further decline among indigenous, Caucasian groups in particular.[8]

My initial response to this data is to say that the churches should not panic. We need to take a long-term view and not a short-term one. The church has grown and declined over centuries, and her experience has been mixed and inevitably so. Personally, I am more concerned with authenticity and identity. The church, in all of her diversity, must be herself first and foremost. If that means that she shrinks numerically, then so be it. If it means that she is out of step with wider culture, then so be it. Jürgen Moltmann, in his book on the cross, identified a dilemma for Christians: either we focus on identity at the expense of relevance, or we accommodate to the cultural context, seeking relevance but

---

8. See the discussion in Cartledge, "British Pentecostalism and Public Theology," 108–23.

at the expense of identity.[9] There is, of course, a tension here. Christianity seeks to live out the gospel in a relevant manner, but not at the expense of its identity in Christ. The religious culture war, especially in the USA, has been politicized such that ideological bundles shape the engagement of Christians with society.[10] This is perhaps less obviously the case in Canada, but it is still present to a greater or lesser degree. How can our distinctive identity as disciples of Christ inform and shape our participation in society as citizens for the common good? This is an important and urgent question for all of the churches in a pluralistic and secularized context.

Building on this question of identity and relevance, or discipleship and citizenship, it is important to consider the role that socialization or "traditioning" plays in the acquisition of religious identity. Socialization refers to the process by which an individual becomes a member of the group, moving from the outside to the inside and eventually becoming an advocate for the group's beliefs and values. For many Christians growing up within a church tradition, this socialization proceeds naturally across the generations, as children and young people are raised within the church's life. However, for many young Christians, they are socialized within a secularized culture as well, leading to what might be termed "faith in two minds." They belong to a secular cultural mind in their public education, which is in tension with their Christian belonging in their congregational settings. These different sets of values mean that a young person is forced to navigate a path between them and often feels more at home in the secular than the Christian world. With the reduced numbers of young Christians in churches, the peer group support is lessened, and this may have a dramatic impact on whether and how young people are retained within the church.

Finally, it is worth noting the impact that congregations have on their local context. Despite the problems noted above, it is still the case that congregations provide a significant amount of social

9. Moltmann, *The Crucified God*.
10. See the discussion by Cartledge and Cartledge, "Pentecostals and Social Engagement," 177–88.

capital within communities, and this benefits them significantly. Social engagement is motivated by faith commitments, and many Christians see their discipleship as being demonstrated in their volunteering and charitable giving outside of the Christian community. This is surely an important point to note. It is the meso-level impact of congregations that is often missed because the analysis of data concentrates on either macro or micro levels of participation. Congregations are an important component in the religious landscape and should be celebrated and resourced by denominations as a significant unit in the maintenance of religious vitality within society.[11]

Conclusion

In this paper, I have reflected on the Canadian census data in the light of my own interests and previous analysis. It is clear that there are significant challenges for the church in contemporary society, and some of these have been identified. Of course, it is always the case that further research is needed to understand the nuances of the big picture that the census data gives. In particular, more research is required to show how the church can resource discipleship for citizenship in an increasingly secularized and pluralistic context such as Canada. I look forward to reading this research in due course.

Bibliography

Brown, Callum G. *The Death of Christian Britain: Understanding Secularization 1800–2000*. 2nd ed. London: Routledge, 2009.

Bruce, Steve. *British Gods: Religion in Modern Britain*. Oxford: Oxford University Press, 2020.

———. *God is Dead: Secularization in the West*. Oxford: Blackwells, 2002

---

11. See Cartledge et al., Megachurches, 333–36.

Cartledge, Mark J., et al. *Megachurches and Social Engagement: Public Theology in Practice.* Leiden: Brill, 2019.

Cartledge, Mark J. and Joan M. Cartledge. "Pentecostals and Social Engagement: Church, Community, and Common Good." In *The Politics of the Spirit: Pentecostal Reflections on Public Responsibility and the Common Good,* edited by Chris Green and Daniela Augustine, 177–88. Lanham, MD: Seymour, 2022.

Cartledge, Mark J. "British Pentecostalism and Public Theology: Navigating the Path between Discipleship and Citizenship." *Journal of the European Pentecostal Theological Association* 41.2 (2021) 108–23.

Casanova, José. *Public Religions in the Modern World.* Chicago: University of Chicago Press, 1994.

Davie, Grace. *Religion in Britain Since 1945.* Oxford, Blackwell, 1994)

———. *The Sociology of Religion.* London: Sage, 2007.

Guest, Matthew. *Neoliberal Religion: Faith and Power in the Twenty-First Century.* London: Bloomsbury Academic, 2022.

Martin, David. *On Secularization: Towards a General Revised General Theory.* Aldershot: Ashgate, 2005.

Moltmann, Jürgen. *The Crucified God.* London: SCM, 1974.

Ziebertz, Hans-Georg, ed. *Religious Individualization and Christian Religious Semantics.* Münster: LIT Verlag, 2001.

THE 2021 CENSUS PANEL: REFLECTION AND RESPONSE

Lee Beach
McMaster Divinity College, Hamilton, ON, Canada

The world is big, and we are small. This is the impression one might be left with when reading the report on religious habits in the 2021 Canadian census and the articles that make up this edition of *Post-Christendom Studies*. If you are a pastor, seminary or Christian college professor, church leader or an interested layperson, it is hard to avoid the idea that the trends reported in the census and reflected on in the articles can leave you feeling like you are tasked with the job of trying to sweep the ocean away with a broom. The trends are large, and they just keep coming with no sense of abatement. They challenge us with questions like: What do we need to know? How do we respond? Thankfully the writers and thinkers who have contributed to this volume have provided both useful analysis of the data and some important thinking on the questions of practice. This article summarizes some of the key ideas that emerge from the various contributions made by the scholars who have contributed to this edition of the journal.

First, there is an overall tenor of hope and optimism that permeates the articles. Despite the reality of demographic trends that speak of a steep decline in the attendance, interest, and overall resources in the traditional church in Canada and every other Western nation, there is a profound sense of hope that the authors offer to us collectively in this issue. For example, Lynne Taylor invites us to see the contextual realities of the Western church as a condition rather than a problem. Problems are something to be solved, but a condition can be a changed circumstance that brings a new reality. It is something that must be worked with rather than solved. Likewise, Stuart Macdonald calls for an honest but hopeful engagement with things as they are as a way forward. There is no hope in trying to reclaim now-long past cultural realities in terms of people's relationship with Christianity. Instead, we must find constructive ways to work with what is in front of us. Mark Noll's article fuels this hopeful disposition when he points out that Christians arguing for a general tolerance of all religions is much more fruitful as a strategy for preserving the place of Christianity than a defense of Christianity as having a special place of privilege. He also points to the development of Indigenous and Hispanic (in the United States) forms of Christianity that are particular to each group and somewhat separate from Western hegemonic forms as a sign of promise.

Each of these is an example of the idea that those who maintain Christian faith today have reason to remain hopeful about the future of the church in society. The job of church leaders is to find ways to cultivate hope in the life of local congregations and faith communities by faithfully communicating a message that reflects a positive future for the church and developing new initiatives that embody the gospel of Christ in ways that are contextually relevant. Even in times of trouble and turmoil, the work of leadership is to provide hope for the future. One cannot read these articles without getting a sense that there is an unmistakable thread of hope that runs through each one of them.

A second and related idea that comes through in the articles is that the church needs to embrace the cultural changes in religious affiliation and work with them and not against them. Anna Robbins is clear on this point when she reminds us that our identity cannot be formed simply by identifying our enemy or by not recognizing that a whole generation of people has been raised in a culture that the 2021 Canadian census reflects. Further, James Robertson avers that perhaps the non-religious today are not abandoning God but rather finding their spiritual desires fulfilled in a way that no longer requires old structures. Jay Mowchenko, drawing on the work of Randy Woodley, goes even further by offering the idea that perhaps the church is in need of a conversion of its own. One that helps it see that it has much to learn from those who identify themselves as "nones" or "dones" and that by opening ourselves up to their experiences and insights, we may find our own faith enriched and our ability to share our faith enhanced.

Mowchenko reflects the wisdom offered in other articles when he writes, "what if the decline of the Christian institutional church in Canada is serving to bring the people of God closer to the posture and mind of Jesus?"[1] This is a provocative but substantial point. It reiterates the need for the church in Post-Christendom to not give in to fear or rail against the "secularizing" powers that prevail on the one hand but then also not fall into a defeatist complacency on the other. Engagement with the world is still the church's calling, but we must work with what we have and where we are rather than wish for something else. These are the times in which we live, and it is a good thing to be here.

Third, and once again building on the previous point, the articles, as a whole, suggest that perhaps this shift may be part of a divine plan in order for the church to rediscover its true identity. Again, Mowchenko is most direct on this point as he wonders about the possibility of whether or not this decline is even meant to be reversed. Could it be that our overarching desire to reverse the downward slide is a sign that we have bought wholeheartedly into the narrative that numbers, abundant resources, and societal influence are the marks of true success? Mark Cartledge says it clearly in his article: "The church has grown and declined over the centuries, and her experience has been mixed and inevitably so. Personally, I am more concerned with authenticity and identity. The church, in all of her diversity, must be herself first and foremost."[2] Perhaps, as in other historical epochs, a time of immense cultural and religious change that seems to be a threat to the Christian faith (or the faith of ancient Israel) can become a time of renewal as the church is forced to reflect on its true identity and beliefs. This kind of reflection can provide a way forward to an even better future if it is done thoughtfully and courageously.

A fourth area of emphasis that a number of the authors explore is the need for the church in Canada, as in other Western countries, to figure out how to better include, respect and work with new immigrants. It is these newcomers whose churches are currently the one overall source of growth for the Christian faith in most, if not

---

1. Found on p. 49 of this edition of *Post-Christendom Studies*.
2. Found on p. 89 of this edition of *Post-Christendom Studies*.

all, Western countries. Sam Reimer's article places some emphasis on this hopeful stream, and Tarus and Barron also provide a robust argument for the need for the Western church to make room for Christians from Africa, Asia, South America, and other places where the church is flourishing. Many of the new immigrants to Canada identify as Christian. It is one thing to celebrate the fact that they start their own churches that reflect their culture and brand of Christian faith; it is quite another for the churches in their new homeland to welcome them and find ways to learn from them and incorporate their gifts and talents into the life and leadership of the local, regional, and national life of the existing church. Of course, there is a live question as to *how* the distinctives of Southern world Christianity are contextually amenable to the global North. But this is an issue to be explored rather than to be feared, and it may also lead to some fresh discoveries about the church's identity and how it can function as its best self.

The general tone of hope, the challenge to embrace the changes, the sense that this may be an opportunity for the church to recover its true calling, and the emphasis on the need to include and work alongside newcomers to Canada are only a few of the themes visible in these essays in *Post-Christendom Studies*. Readers could point to any number of others, such as how churches will respond to the LGBTQ+ issue and how this may contribute to how they are perceived in society as a whole. These are part of a much larger conversation that will require more reflection moving forward.

Simply put, the downward trend in religious affiliation is likely to continue. When Statistics Canada releases its 2031 census results, it seems improbable that the data will show anything other than more of the same. The church needs to evaluate and reflect on how it would like to respond. If the responses here are any indication, however, we should remain confident that there is a path forward—even if the world is big, and we are small.

BOOK REVIEW

Rolnick, Philip A. *A Post-Christendom Faith: The Long Battle For The Human Soul.* Waco. Texas: Baylor University Press, 2021. x+125 pp. Hardcover, ISBN: 9781481308922. $46.95.

In his first installment of a three-volume work, Philip Rolnick takes a historical look at the ongoing quest for the human soul. Wide in scope, the book employs the *theory of unintended consequences* regarding Luther's *Ninety-Five Theses*. Extending from the Reformation to its unavoidable end, Luther's Pandora's Box spawned an array of theologies and ideologies that ultimately ended with a critique of the existence of God; what remains in the box, we must assume, will be revealed in volumes two and three and will conclude (to some extent) *The Long Battle for the Human Soul*.

Rolnick's book postulates three Epochal Events. The first, the Reformation—due to the eventual multiplicity of Christian claims—led to the Enlightenment (the Second Epochal Event). Enlightenment thought necessitated a new way of explaining existence that spawned the scientific method, whose literary arm, the historical-critical method, turned its discerning eye on the Bible and gave rise to Secularism and Atheism. The third Epochal Event, the French Revolution, moved away from the Bible's teachings because human progress was now antithetical to Christianity. The Revolution descended into warfare and mass slaughter, as did similar revolutions to come—including the Leninist-Stalinist, Maoist, and Hitlerian. Rolnick tips his hand at the eventual direction of volumes two and three when he points out that human brotherhood movements (revolutions), without God's fatherhood, predictably failed.

These Epochal events led to Christianity's critique, attack, or eschewal with its eventual replacement by Atheism, Romanticism, Nihilism, and Positivism. Atheism's full voice was found in its champion Friedrich Nietzsche. Nietzsche believed faith in God to be harmful to human progress and, therefore, must be condemned. Nietzsche attacked and dissected faith, morality, and the concepts of good and bad; he treated them as tools of the weak that can only be overcome through the *will to power* of the Ubermensch—humanity's one true goal. Rolnick correctly points out that Nietzsche's denial of God's transcendence, truth, and morality has shaped contemporary attitudes and beliefs.

Although the book can be weighty at times, its strength lies in the revelatory notion of the totality of what Luther put into motion. Many understand the Reformation as ending in Anabaptism (or even the Roman Catholic Reformation), but Rolnick allows the reader to see that its ultimate end is neither the aforementioned or Atheism nor the inevitable questioning of God's existence but ends with the question of existence itself—as in the writings of Hume, Descartes, and the theory of quantum entanglement that all question, thought, reality, and our existence—all this from Luther's objections to the Catholic Church's abuses.

In the end, Rolnick rightly points out that "for all the increasingly open attacks on Christianity and its founder," and just like the multiplicity of belief systems in the first century, countless millions continued to believe "trusting their lives were laden with meaning and eternal value." The first volume of the *Long Battle for the Human Soul* underlines the fact that the goal of the Reformation, and all that followed, was to protect and secure the human soul. In his final statement of this volume, Rolnick makes it plain that the gospel is the solution to the long battle of the human soul; how he delineates this is much anticipated. Rolnick's book is a welcomed and illuminating addition to the scholarship on post-Christendom culture.

Dudley A. Brown
Independent Scholar
Cambridge, ON

BOOK REVIEW

Kim, Ted. *Save Europe: Reintroducing Christianity to Post-Christian Europe*, Eugene, OR: Resource Publications, 2021, xvi+207 pp. ISBN: 978-1-7252-7933-9. $26.00.

In his thought-provoking work, *Save Europe: Reintroducing Christianity to Post-Christian Europe*, Ted Kim—a theologian whose church-planting efforts have led to the baptism of over a thousand individuals—passionately contends that a revival of Christianity in Europe hinges upon the reintroduction of Jesus Christ: the gospel. Since spirituality is at the core of the continent's contemporary dilemmas, Kim argues that such a revival is crucial for a continent grappling with an identity crisis, as it holds the potential to provide Europeans with a "meaningful relationship with the living God" (xii).

The book is structured into twelve chapters, each offering a unique perspective on the revival of Christianity in Europe. He begins by exploring the concept of "Europe as a Major Mission Field." He asserts that European intellectuals, including figures such as Nietzsche, set in motion a gradual spiritual decline by proclaiming the death of God. This proclamation ultimately led to the rise of secularism, an unsettling spiritual condition that has long gone unaddressed; however, in this uncertain context, Kim sees this as an opportunity, through faith, for Christians to disseminate the gospel. At the height of their spiritual zeal, European Christian missionaries spread the gospel worldwide, driven by what Kim sees as a misinterpretation of Matt 24:14, "This gospel of the kingdom would be preached in the whole world as a testimony to all nations, and then the end will come." They believed this would precipitate the Second Advent. Unfortunately—and ironically—this enthusiasm contributed to the erosion of Christian influence within Europe. Kim interprets this passage differently, emphasizing that "God will not end history until all humanity has had the opportunity to hear the gospel" (20). Consequently, Kim advocates for a second global dissemination of the gospel.

He underscores the notion that contemporary Europeans "are not the same people who slid away from Christianity in the prior generations" (23), asserting that Jesus extends multiple opportunities for redemption. Kim supports this argument through biblical examples of "repetition" and narratives, such as the healing of the blind man at Bethsaida, Peter's denial of Jesus, the story of John Mark, and the parables of the lost sheep, the lost coin, and the prodigal son. He then looks at the "explosion of freedom—culturally, morally and psychologically" and the lasting effects of the sexual revolution of the 1960s on the decline of Christianity in Europe (34). Kim proposes that reversing this trend requires a reintroduction of Jesus "based on a more candid understanding of human nature," as only Jesus possesses the depth of insight needed (38).

Kim also emphasizes the necessity for Europeans to embrace the exclusivity of Jesus as the sole savior of the world, facilitated by the power of the Holy Spirit, without giving "credence to the submission to Allah as the condition for salvation" (122). He succinctly summarizes various challenges facing Christianity, ranging from the interaction between science and religion to the interplay of intellect and faith and addressing topics such as God, wealth, sexuality, LGBT+ issues, Islam, and religious pluralism.

After diagnosing the problem, Kim explores the restoration of Christianity in post-Christian Europe. As a framing device, he contends that Christianity began as a "post-Christ" event guided by the Holy Spirit that emerged *after* Jesus's ascension into heaven. He urges against reinventing Christianity and instead advocates drawing lessons from its history. For evidence, he points to unsuccessful attempts at reinvention in the past, such as Universalism/Unitarianism, monasticism, evangelicalism, the Jesus People, and non-church movements. With his focus on restoring the gospel, Kim even proposes that European churches could disband and restart with a renewed focus on preaching the "good news" of Jesus as the only means of salvation. Given Europe's material wealth, financial support would be unnecessary; instead, it would require adept religious guidance to address the perceived spiritual malnourishment. Prospective Christian missionaries in this context must be intellectuals who "understand the postmodern western mindset" (171). The final chapter encourages Europe to draw inspiration from the United States, particularly in fostering spiritual revival. While cautioning against blind nationalism, Kim highlights the American experience of nurturing the Christian landscape through revivals and self-critique. He calls upon Europeans to pray for contemporary spiritual leaders and intellectuals who can reintroduce Christianity effectively.

Kim's study lacks a clear delineation of the geographical boundaries concerning his subject, Europe, a continent comprising approximately 44 countries, including Russia. While the objective is commendable, it is, in practical terms, a difficult proposition, and Kim's missionary strategies seem somewhat antiquated. Unfortunately, this oversight results in inadequate attention to Russia. Europe's rich cultural diversity presents a multifaceted challenge, and Kim's proposal for a universal remedy in reintroducing Christianity occasionally appears triumphalist and overly idealistic. For example, what may succeed in Belgium cannot necessarily be transposed into the Polish context. Establishing a precise definition of Europe would significantly enhance our comprehension of Kim's central thesis: the reintroduction of Christianity in a post-Christian Europe.

While Kim encourages Europeans to draw insights from the religious experience of the United States, it is crucial to exercise caution. The religious landscape of the US differs significantly from that of Europe. The US, characterized by Kim as the envy of the world (173), is a single country with English as its official language. In contrast, Europe encompasses numerous countries with distinct cultures, religions, and spirituality. These profound disparities make it challenging for Europe's religious transformation to emulate that of the US.

Furthermore, the author's argument revolves around the reintroduction of the gospel, which he simplifies as "Jesus." Notably, Kim allocates minimal attention to elements such as the virgin birth and the sinless life of Jesus, which are pivotal in supporting his contention regarding the exclusivity of Jesus as the sole savior of the world, particularly in Europe, where Christianity competes with other Abrahamic monotheistic religions.

In the same vein, Kim overlooks the profound impact of Christian economic immigrants from sub-Saharan Africa, the epicenter of Christianity. These indigenous African immigrants, encompassing both Christians and Muslims, exhibit a deep religiosity. However, the author predominantly addresses the latter group while neglecting the former. Ironically, these economically motivated Christian immigrants are instrumental in establishing some of the largest churches in Europe. Notable examples include Sunday Adelajah's church in Kyiv, Ukraine, and Matthew Ashimolow's church in London. These thriving churches were founded by indigenous sub-Saharan immigrants, highlighting a compelling facet of Europe's evolving religious landscape.

Kim underscores the importance of prayer, faith, and the reintroduction of Jesus—the book's central thesis—in Europe's spiritual revitalization. He advocates for the establishment of conservative and evangelical theological seminaries. Kim's arguments exude a dated quality, and his assertion that we should refrain from reimagining the faith is indeed commendable but may come across as somewhat antiquated. His proposition that Christians, or perhaps missionaries, should merely reintroduce Christ to Europe also seems rooted in an attraction-based model of ministry that lacks contemporary effectiveness, raising questions about its viability in the future. While *Save Europe* may be helpful reading for graduate students and theologians interested in missions, it should be noted that the text contains numerous typographical errors and could benefit from using gender-neutral language.

Paul S. Chimhungwe
Kgolagano College of Theological Education
Gaborone, Botswana

BOOK REVIEW

Jenkins, Philip. *Fertility and Faith: The Demographic Revolution and the Transformation of World Religions*. Waco: Baylor University Press, 2020. 262 pp. ISBN 978-1481311311. $34.99.

Pastors and congregants who are alarmed by the empty pews on Sunday will find Philip Jenkins's *Fertility and Faith* a helpful resource on why those pews are so vacant. It will, perhaps, also alleviate some guilt as to who is to "blame" for the decline of attendance or the shuttering of empty churches—the cause is something much larger than just poor sermons, old music, or mediocre programs.

Philip Jenkins is a Distinguished Professor of History at Baylor University. He is a recognized academic (30 books to his credit) and a public intellectual who engages with a number of pressing issues. He is most recognized for his attention to trends within global Christianity and, to a lesser degree, other faiths. *Fertility and Faith* further develops his earlier (and "classic") work *The Next Christendom* (2002), along with *The New Faces of Christianity* (2006) and *God's Continent* (2007). Jenkins has a unique ability to make sense of a host of statistics related to trends and trajectories and provide insightful and irenic suggestions for constructively moving forward in light of such complexities.

It is obvious that church decline in the West is caused by a host of interconnected factors, one of which is what is commonly called secularism. Jenkins's claim is that the churches' decline (and rising secularism) cannot be understood without considering demography. Stated simply, there is a link between secularism, church decline, and fertility.

In typical Jenkins fashion, the book makes a compelling case with copious statistics and insightful analysis. In Part I, he explores the way in which the decline of the Western church beginning in the 1960s was paralleled by the rapid decline of the Total Fertility Rate (TFR; measurement of how many children a woman will have over the course of her lifetime). For a society to maintain its current population, a TFR rate needs to be 2.1. Since the 1960s, nations within the West have gone from a postwar Baby Boom to a Baby Bust, a TFR that has dropped from numbers above 5.0 to below 2.0. The numbers range up and down according to nation, but the trend is clear—Western nations are in numerical decline, with some nations bringing in immigrants to counter the trend, and others (such as Japan) declining in population rather than changing their culture with the arrival of large numbers of foreigners.

Concurrent with the decline of the TFR was a rise in secularism. Jenkins provides a host of details and statistics on the decline of the church in the West, and the concomitant rise of secularism. His aim is to argue that there is a link between secularism and low fertility (a TFR under 2.1)—but is humble in acknowledging that the link is observable but not entirely demonstratable. Stated differently, the link is clear, but, as he notes, correlation is not causation: "The fact that the two phenomena, demographic and religious, tracked so well together does not of itself prove causation. But the more we examine the process of religious transformation, the more unavoidable becomes the demographic interpretation" (49).

The reasons for the decline of TFR are many, some major ones being advanced education for women, increasing numbers of women in the workforce, and birth control options. In places marked by such dynamics, the TFR declines precipitously. And secularism goes up.

He spends a chapter exploring the supposed anomaly of the United States, often seen as a modern, industrial, and well-educated nation that has bucked the telos of secularism. However, he makes a compelling argument that secularizing trends seen in Western places such as Europe, Canada, Australia, New Zealand, and South Korea are beginning to show in the US, suggesting that the US did not avoid the impact of such trends but was merely a generation or two behind the curve.

Part II of the book explores global trends outside of the Western world, and Jenkins develops a compelling case for the link between demography, religion, and political trajectories, both within the global church but also with the world of Islam, Hinduism, and Judaism. His work is finely tuned to religion and region, and I encourage readers to go through the details in his book. Here are a few summary points worth considering. While the church in the West struggles with a replacement rate TFR, the church in sub-Saharan Africa has a booming TFR that continues to fill the pews to overflowing. And since there is a correlation between fertility and faith, such regions are probably not going to be facing Western-style secularism anytime soon. The chapter on Islam reveals that much of the world of Islam has an exceedingly high TFR—much like the church in sub-Saharan Africa—making inroads of secularism unlikely. That rapid demographic growth beside and among a ballooning African church may, he suggests, lead to further and more troubling clashes between the two faiths. However, Jenkins does note some Muslim-majority nations have already begun to have a much lower TFR, such as Iran with a TFR as low as 1.66. It is such striking declines of TFR that leads to Jenkin raising questions about the arrival of secularism and a decline of faith in the world of Islam.

The final chapter in Part II links demography with politics, and more specifically populism in Israel, Turkey, India, and Russia. Be it the rise or decline of Islam, Hinduism, Judaism, or Christianity, there will inevitably be consequences on the political front. Jenkins refers to US President Lyndon Johnson's quip about politicians needing to "be able to count" as a springboard for noting how populism in the above-noted nations is marked by fears or hopes related to the demographic growth of one's allies or enemies. Not understanding demography, he argues, will leave one in the dark as to what is really going on in such places.

The final chapter is a brief examination of what the church (or any religion for that matter) needs to do when facing a TFR below replacement rate. A church filled with elderly people is the inevitable endgame of such demography, and churches need to adjust accordingly. In fact, a church that does not adjust to an aging society, women in the workforce, and fewer children, will hasten its own demise.

I have never read a book by Jenkins that I did not like. And that is the case for this volume. I highly recommend anyone interested in the decline of the church in the West—or the state of the global church (or other religions)—read this valuable work.

Gordon L. Heath
McMaster Divinity College
Hamilton, ON

BOOK REVIEW

Reimer, Sam. *Caught in the Current: British and Canadian Evangelicals in an Age of Self-Spirituality.* Montreal and Kingston: McGill-Queen's University Press, 2023. xiii + 231 pp. ISBN 9780228016960. $34.95.

In this illuminating volume, Sam Reimer uses his extensive background studying evangelicalism in Canada and Great Britain to elucidate how the beliefs and practices of evangelical Christians are being shaped by "the rejection of institutional religious authority, and the relocation of authority inside the individual" (15). Reimer, who serves as Professor of Sociology at Crandall University, weaves together cultural commentary and excerpts from interviews and survey data to paint a compelling picture of the state of evangelical churches amid significant changes to the undercurrents of Western culture.

After a brief introduction that reviews the core argument and structure of the book, Reimer advances his foundational point regarding a change in loci of authority in chapter one. Reimer argues that the predominant cultural posture towards religion is now self-spirituality, whereby a crisis of legitimacy has caused people throughhout the Western world to consider themselves, as individuals, to be the only legitimate authority or arbiter of what one ought to believe and how one ought to live (24, 29). Self-spirituality, therefore, helps complexify the growth of a "you do you" posture towards religion, particularly within evangelicalism. This initial chapter is foundational for the rest of the book, as its arguments are used as a touch point for discussing how the changing loci of authority—from external sources to internal—is problematizing various elements of evangelicalism and the Christian faith more broadly.

In chapters two through four, Reimer investigates how the authority of the self has problematized notions of orthodoxy, orthopraxy, and faith transmission. For orthodoxy (chapter two), Reimer argues that beliefs are becoming less propositional and "more about statements of belonging and identity," whereby relationships play an increasingly important role in the formation of beliefs (54–55). On a host of theological and ethical issues explored in the chapter, a consistent theme emerges of interviewees expressing their convictions cautiously to ensure they are understood as not attempting to impose themselves on another person (and, thereby, on another's individuality). Likewise, the cautious approach evangelicals take in communicating their beliefs was also expressed in their orthopraxy (chapter three), such that devotional practices, church attendance, volunteerism, charity, and evangelism are all being redefined in light of an inner locus of authority that seeks personal authenticity above all other considerations. Given these changes to how the faithful understand belief and practice, it should not be surprising that faith transmission (chapter four) has become serpentine and wrought with issues. In an age of self-spirituality, not only is religious adherence assumed to be primarily about the transmission of morals (126, 129), but the adoption of the faith is tacitly and increasingly understood as an abuse of power by the parent (or clergy) who is stifling the individuality of the child or as an abdication of responsibility by the child to find or define themselves (129).

In chapters five and six, Reimer explores how self-spirituality is shaping the evangelical subculture and postures toward politics and denominationalism. While comparatively weaker than the other chapters, Reimer effectively teases out some of the differences and similarities between Canadian, American, and, to a lesser extent, British evangelicalism. Indeed, Canadian and British evangelicalism often share a similar posture of cautious suspicion towards American evangelicals and are generally much less connected to a specific political party. Canadian and British evangelicals, it seems, will vote according to policy no matter the party more readily than their American counterparts. Likewise, evangelicals have diminishing affinity with the denominational structures of old, preferring network ecclesiology that is (comparably) unfettered by bureaucracy and offers more freedom to experiment.

One of the key strengths of this work is how it has been structured. In each chapter, Reimer weaves cultural analysis with interview and survey data and, in doing so, convincingly supports and substantiates his cultural commentary. The movement between theory and practice this weaving implies convincingly shows how self-spirituality shapes Canadian and British evangelicalism today and makes the book engaging and thought-provoking. Furthermore, Reimer effectively balances the melancholy that arises when discussing substantial cultural changes and their effects on the church (particularly church decline) with genuine hope and an invitation to see these changes as opportunities rather than obstacles. In this way, the book describes the current state of affairs while inviting evangelicals to consider how to adjust (as we have done in the past) to our changing cultural circumstances.

However, there are two areas for improvement in the volume related to its core argument: anemic discussions regarding what authority is and the underlying role of postmodernism in the shift of authority the book describes. Taking only one paragraph (22), Reimer's definition of authority as legitimate power does not, in my view, appropriately complexify the issues of authority discussed throughout the volume. Basing his definition on that of Max Weber, Reimer does not discuss Weber's (modernist) complexification of his definition, whereby Weber argued for a tripartite classification of types of authority (traditional, rational, and charismatic). Doing so reveals the necessarily modernist bent of Weber's definition, which raises the question of whether the definition still makes sense in the era after modernity. While this does not significantly harm the book's argument, it does leave a considerable line of cultural exegesis open that would have strengthened the arguments made throughout. To be sure, this is why I also raise the issue of postmodernism's exclusion because extrapolating the implications of postmodernism (and the emerging tensions of metamodernism) would have offered a thread that ties each part of the volume together and would help Reimer more thoroughly reflect on the nature of authority in the twenty-first century. For example, part of the postmodern condition is the deconstruction of hierarchies due to a suspicion of inherent power differentials implied by their structure. As hierarchies are deconstructed, so is the conceptual framework by which authority as a metaphor functions, making authority an increasingly incoherent concept. Moreover, once all hierarchies are deconstructed, only the individual is left. Indeed, the authority-of-the-self implied by self-spirituality is, in essence, using the concept of hierarchy (authority) to assert a fascinating narcissistic oxymoron—but it is one that makes sense in light of the postmodern condition. All of this helps to explain, on a cultural level, why self-spirituality is exerting itself and points to the fact that the movement from external to internal loci of authority is not a distinct cultural development but the consequence of already well-known but poorly understood developments (modernism, postmodernism, secularism; and lesser known, such as metamodernism and hyperculture).

Even still, *Caught in the Current* is an excellent description of and reflection on the cultural undercurrents informing many of the challenges evangelicals—and, indeed, all Christians living in the West—face in the contemporary age. This book will benefit academics and pastors alike, as by describing the crucial underlying element of the issues we face, Reimer has given a new perspective from which the church can begin to pivot and respond in constructive, kingdom-building ways.

Seán McGuire
Wentworth Baptist Church
Hamilton, ON

MODERN AUTHORS INDEX

Adogame, A., 79
Airhart, P. D., 9

Beach, L., 34, 79
Bechsgaard, G., 71
Bediako, K., 74
Berger, P., 16
Bethune, A. N., 36–37, 38–39, 41–42, 45
Bibby, R. W., 7
Bramadat, P., 76
Brown, C. G., 87
Bruce, S., 97
Bullivant, S., 14
Byassee, J., 69

Campbell, H., 17
Carpenter, J. A., 74
Cartledge, J., 90
Cartledge, M. J., 88, 89, 90
Carwana, B., 16
Casanova, J., 87
Chalmers, G., 38, 42
Chaves, M., 16
Clarke, B., 6–7, 14, 29–30, 32, 68
Collins, J., 48
Cornelissen, L., 29

Davie, G., 87
Davis, J., 34

Dawn, M. J., 49
Dilmaghani, M., 69
Duff, M., 67
Durie, M. H., 67

Fitch, D., 66
Fitz-Gerald, J., 78
Flatt, K., 32
Fountain, P., 67

Gordon, J., 78
Gornik, M. R., 79
Graham, M., 34
Guest, M., 88
Guretzki, D., 79

Hanciles, J. J., 74, 75, 78
Harris, B., 66
Hastings, A., 75
Heath, E., 51, 53
Heath, G. L., 23
Hiemstra, R., 14, 15, 22, 50

Inglehart, R., 15

Janzen, R., 79
Jenkins, P., 74, 76–77
Johnstone, P., 74

Kiser, C., 51, 53
Kreider, A., 53

Kubler-Ross, E., 50
Kwiyani, H. C., 79

Lacasse, S., 29
LeBlanc, T., 59
Lewis, J., 22
Lockhart, R. A., 69
Loftin, M., 49–50
Los, J., 36

Macdonald, S., 6–7, 14, 29–30, 32, 68
Marks, L., 69
Martin, D., 87
Mbiti, J. S., 76, 80
McCann, G., 71
McDonald, B., 68
Moir, J. S., 39, 42
Moltmann, J., 90
Mountain, J., 41

Newbigin, L., 75
Noll, M. A., 55

Ogot, B. A., 76

Pennings, R., 36
Powell, R., 69

Reimer, S., 14, 15, 16, 17, 22, 77
Reyngoud, A., 68
Romero, R. C., 59

Ryerson, E., 40, 43–44

Sanneh, L., 74
Sawyerr, H., 80–81
Schmidt, C., 23
Snyder, T., 36
Stackhouse, J. G., 56
Stiller, K., 50
Strachan, J., 39, 40
Stuart, J., 39–40, 42

Taylor, C., 17, 67
Taylor, L., 70
Thiessen, J., 7, 11–12
Thompson, N., 36
Tillich, P., 25
Troughton, G., 67

Van Pelt, D., 58

Walls, A. F., 74, 75–76, 80
Watts, G., 17
Webster, D., 18
Welbourn, F. B., 76
Wilkins-Laflamme, S., 11–12
Witte, J., 58
Wittmeier, B., 78
Woodley, R., 51–53

Ziebertz, H., 88
Zurlo, G. A., 76, 77

www.ingramcontent.com/pod-product-compliance
Lightning Source LLC
Chambersburg PA
CBHW071223160426
43196CB00012B/2389